HUNGARIAN BUSINESS LAW

Hungarian Business Law

by

Dr. Klara Oppenheim

and

Jenny Power, Esq.

Counsels of
Heller, Löber, Bahn & Partners
Vienna – Budapest – Prague

Kluwer Law and Taxation Publishers
Deventer • Boston

Kluwer Law and Taxation Publishers
P.O. Box 23   Tel. : 31-5700-47261
7400 GA Deventer   Telex: 49295
The Netherlands   Fax   : 31-5700-22244

Library of Congress Cataloging in Publication Data

Oppenheim, Klara.
Hungarian Business Law/by Klara Oppenheim and Jenny Power.
p.   cm.
ISBN 9065444904
1. Business enterprises—Hungary.   2. Business enterprises—
Taxation—Hungary.   3. Trade regulation—Hungary.   I. Power,
Jenny.   II. Title.
KKF1040.O66   1990
346.439'07—dc20
[344.39067]   90–4686
                                                       CIP

Cover design: Boudewijn Betzema

ISBN 90 6544 490 4

Table of Contents

Chapter 5
Activities requiring government permission

Chapter 6
Companies operating in duty-free zones

Chapter 7
Special regulations concerning foreign participation

Chapter 8

Chapter 9

Chapter 12

Chapter 13

Introduction

The rate of progress of reform in Hungary over the last ten years has been dazzling. As Hungary moves further toward developing a free market economy, foreign businessmen are increasingly prospecting in Hungary and discovering significant opportunities.

Hungary has developed the legal framework for the foundation of up-to-date forms of economic association. The Act VI of 1988 on Economic Associations, the Act XXIV of 1988 on Foreign Investments in Hungary and the Act XIII of 1989 on Transformation of Economic Organizations and Economic Associations may be considered the three basic statutes of Hungarian business law. Together with the related tax regulations and administrative rules they facilitate the establishment of a free market, in particular by lifting the bars which had previously separated the socialist sector from the so-called private sector. They guarantee equal rights and obligations for all economic ventures and provide certain tax incentives for foreign participation, thereby promoting the investment of the foreign working capital into the Hungarian economy. In contrast to the situation before the reforms, the supervision of the Registration Courts eliminates the possibility of the state's direct intervention, and the normative registration system puts an end to the possibility of individual judgments.

This book is designed mainly to provide foreigners interested in investing in Hungary with information about the rather complicated Hungarian legal system. For this purpose emphasis is placed on the forms of economic association available to foreigners under Hungarian business law and the most important tax rules related to them.

As Hungary's efforts towards developing a free market economy are continuous and on-going, there have been frequent modifications to the company regulations in recent months and the process can be expected to continue for some time. This book presents the legal situation in Hungary as of 1 March 1990.

Chapter 1

Forms of doing business in Hungary

1.1 General

The Act VI of 1988 on Economic Associations (hereinafter also referred to as the 'Company Act'), the basic legislation concerning economic associations, mandates that economic associations may be established only pursuant to this Act.

As in most other jurisdictions, Hungarian corporate law distinguishes between doing business in legal forms involving the personal liability of the entrepreneur and forms in which a corporate entity serves as a shelter for the shareholders to avoid personal liability for the debts of the company. Conceptually then, the economic associations may be divided into two groups according to the liability of the members.

1.2 Forms with unlimited liability

The following forms of 'unlimited liability companies' are available:
- unlimited partnership
- economic working community
- deposit partnership
- business union
- joint enterprise.

The common feature of all these types is that the members of the economic associations are liable for the obligations of the company with all their private assets.

1.3 Forms with limited liability

The 'limited liability companies' are as follows:
- limited liability company (kft)
- public company limited by shares (rt).

The members of the economic associations belonging to this second group are liable only to the extent of their contribution to the company.

Since it is a reasonable desire of investors to limit their business risks, foreign investors generally choose one of the forms of companies with limited liability.

1.4 Other forms

Although the Company Act emphasizes that economic associations may be founded only in the forms enumerated above, some regulations have remained in force authorizing the establishment of the following enterprises:
- cooperatives, including small cooperatives, cooperatives of small manufacturers and social associations
- water management associations and civil law associations
- agricultural unions.

The Company Act does not govern these forms, and since economic associations with foreign participation may be founded only in a way and form regulated by this Act, they should not be of particular interest to the foreign investor.

Chapter 2

The limited liability company: Kft

2.1 Foundation of the company

2.1.1 General

A limited liability company is referred to in Hungarian as Korlátolt felelösségü társaság or by the abbreviation Kft.

2.1.2 The founders

A limited liability company may be formed by natural persons and legal entities without any limitation. Formerly, a foreign entity was entitled to participate in the establishment of an economic association only if it qualified as a firm according to its domestic law or if it was entered in a register of firms. This rule did not apply for public companies limited by shares, since foreign natural persons were permitted to be shareholders. According to the Regulation on Private Entrepreneurs, these restrictions are no longer effective as of 1 April 1990.

While the Company Act generally prescribes at least two parties for the foundation of an economic association, a limited liability company may be founded by one member only ('one-man company'). The limited liability company is different from the public company limited by shares in the sense that it is a form which enables its members to unite the capital and personal efforts of its members.

2.1.3 The stock capital

The limited liability company is an association formed with stock capital consisting of the original contributions of the individual members. This contribution is referred to in the Company Act as the 'primary stake' in order to distinguish this from the member's percentage interest in the company which is referred to as his 'quota'. The stock capital of the company cannot be less than HUF 1,000,000. This capital can be made available both in cash and in kind with the limitation that the cash contribution cannot be less than 30 per cent of the stock capital and not less than HUF 500,000 at the foundation of the company. The primary stakes of the members may differ but may not be less than HUF 100,000 each. Each primary stake must be expressed in forints and be exactly divisible by HUF 10,000.

No company member may be exempted from payment of the capital contribution and no set-off is permitted. Any provision to the contrary in the articles of association is invalid. The purpose of this provision is to ensure that the stock capital be real and not fictious.

The in-kind contributions have to be made fully available by the time of the registration of the company, while a grace period is permitted for the payment of the cash contributions such that half of each primary stake may be paid in by the time of the registration of the company and the other half – but at least HUF 500,000 – within one year from the time of registration. In the case of a one-man company the cash contribution also has to be made fully available to the company by the time of registration.

2.1.4 Contributions in kind

Any negotiable asset with a real value, any intellectual property and any valuable right can be an in-kind contribution.

The evaluation of an in-kind contribution is sometimes a problem. If the company is required to have an auditor, it is forbidden to attribute a higher value to an in-kind contribution than that fixed by the auditor.

The Company Act decrees that a member supplying a contribution in kind bears liability for a period of five years from the date of such contribution that the value of his contribution indeed equalled, at the time of deposit, the value indicated in the articles of association.

2.1.5 Subsidiary contributions

In addition to providing their primary stakes, the members of the company may undertake to supply other valuable contributions, known as subsidiary contributions. Although personal participation in the operation of the company, referred to in the Company Act as personal collaboration, is not mandatory in the case of a limited liability company, it is permitted. Unless the personal collaboration is performed by a member as an elected official (i.e. as a member of the supervisory board or as a manager), this activity is deemed to be such a subsidiary contribution. It is valued as equal to the work of an external person for which remuneration is due *ex lege*. This remuneration is entered in the company's balance sheet among the liabilities, even if it has to be paid from the stock capital.

2.2 Additional payment

Although it is a principal rule that a member is liable only up to the amount of his primary stake, the Company Act provides one possibility for additional liability. Any additional payment may only be prescribed by the articles of association and is solely for the purpose of covering losses of the company. It does not, then, constitute an increase in the stock capital. The articles of association must also stipulate the amount of the additional payment, either in figure or in percentage. The additional payment must be made in proportion to each member's primary stake and does not increase the member's quota. Any portion of the additional payment no longer necessary for covering the losses has to be refunded to the members.

2.3 Quota

The members may not reclaim their original contribution or primary stakes during the existence of the company. During the existence of the company the members are, rather, entitled to so-called quotas, which represent the totality of the membership rights and obligations of each member. The value of the quota is not fixed but fluctuates with its market value. Quotas may be freely transferred only to the members of the company and may not be assigned to a non-member until the member has fully paid in his primary stake. The other members of the company, the company itself and the person designated by the members' meeting have, in this order, a right to buy the quota under the same conditions as offered by an outside person. The company may buy up to one-third of the quotas from its assets exceeding the stock capital. According to the Company Act the articles of association may not stipulate more favorable conditions for the transfer of quotas than those indicated above.

2.4 Increase and decrease of primary capital

There is a possibility to increase or decrease the stock capital of the limited liability company. The increase may be effected not only by the investment of new primary stakes, but also by converting assets of the company beyond the stock capital into stock capital. In this latter case the amount of the quotas will be increased proportionally.

The members' meeting may decide on a decrease of the stock capital taking into consideration the provision of the Company Act regulating the minimum amount of the primary stake and the formal rules safeguarding creditors' interests.

2.5 The corporate organs

A limited liability company must have at least a members' meeting and a manager. In those cases defined in the Company Act a supervisory board and an auditor are also obligatory.

2.5.1 The members' meeting

The members' meeting is the supreme corporate organ of the limited liability company. The Company Act enumerates the matters belonging to the exclusive competence of the members' meeting, including:
– examination and approval of the balance sheet and the distribution of profits;
– decreeing additional payments to the company itself to cover losses of the company and repayment of the same;

7

- division and withdrawal of a business share;
- exclusion of a member;
- election and recall of managers, determination of their renumeration and exercise of employers' rights in respect to the managers;
- election and recall of the members of the supervisory board as well as their renumeration, except as further stipulated in the Company Act;
- approval of the conclusion of contracts in which the value of the contract exceeds one-quarter of the stock capital of the company as well as all contracts to be concluded between the company and one of its own members, managers or one of their close relatives, except where the conclusion of such contract is within the usual course of business activities of a company;
- approval of contracts concluded on behalf of the company prior to its registration;
- claims for damages against members responsible for the foundation of the company, managers and the members of the supervisory board;
- decisions concerning termination, transformation or merger of the company;
- modification of the articles of association.

No departure from these provisions in the articles of association is considered valid.

In the case of a one-man company the competence of the members' meeting is exercised by the founder.

Resolutions are generally passed by a simple majority of votes, except as otherwise regulated in the articles of association, and each member has at least ten votes. The logic of this provision of the Company Act is that the minimum amount of primary stake held by a shareholder is HUF 100,000, while according to another, although not mandatory provision of the Company Act, each HUF 10,000 of primary stake entitles the holder to one vote. The extent of the voting rights and the procedure to be followed in case of a tied vote must be regulated in the articles of association.

The members' meeting has a quorum when at least half of the stock capital is represented in the meeting.

The members' meeting must be called at least once a year and, unless otherwise provided in the articles of association, this is done by the managers. A members' meeting must be called whenever it is necessary in the interests of the company and must probably be called whenever it becomes apparent from the company's balance sheet that stock capital has been reduced by half owing to losses.

2.5.2 The manager

2.5.2.1 Definition

One or more managers serve as the managing, executive and representative organ of the limited liability company. The manager executes the business policy and management decisions. The manager is also responsible to see to it that the company keeps all necessary company books and must further prepare the balance sheet and inventory of assets of the company and submit these to the members' meeting.

2.5.2.2 Employment

The manager is a natural person who is either a member of the company or an external person. In both cases the manager of the company may work pursuant to a labor contract or on a commission basis without being an employee of the company. If he is employed, the activities of the manager are governed by the Labor Code except in respect to liability which is – according to the Company Act – unlimited for any damage caused by breach of duty as defined by the rules of the Civil Code.

2.5.2.3 The number of managers

The first manager must be named in the articles of association. The articles of association may further determine the number of the managers to be elected, but may also stipulate that each member of the company is entitled to management and representation. In such a case all the members are deemed to be managers.

In case of a one-man company the deed of foundation may empower the founder for management.

2.5.2.4 Conflict of interest

The Company Act refers to a manager as a 'leading official' and declares that one person may be the leading official of two economic associations at the same time and then provides certain rules concerning conflicts of interest, referred to as rules of incompatibility. Only with the consent of the members' meeting may the manager:
– carry on any business-like economic activity falling within the company's range of activities;
– be an unlimited-liability partner in another economic association carrying on similar activities; or
– be a leading official in another economic association pursuing similar activities.
In contrast, in case of a public company limited by shares, the members of the board of directors and supervisory board are completely precluded from such activities.

In the event the manager engages in any of these prohibited activities, the company has the following options:
– to claim damages;
– to demand in lieu of damages that the manager release the company from the transaction concluded on his own behalf; or
– to demand that he surrender to the company any profits arising out of the transaction.

2.5.2.5 Representation of the company

The manager represents the company in all in- and out-of-court matters. Where the limited liability company has more than one manager, they are entitled to jointly represent the company, however, the articles of association may depart from this rule and entitle each manager to represent the company alone. The manager may transfer the right of representation for a determined class of affairs to the employees of the company.

The manager's right of representation may be limited internally, but such a limitation has no effect with respect to third persons.

The articles of association must stipulate the same extent for the right of representation as for the right to sign on behalf of the firm (e.g. the manager may not be granted an unlimited right to represent the company and a limited right to sign on behalf of the company). The managers may either individually or jointly represent and sign. If there are more than two managers, one of them (appointed by name) may represent and sign individually, while the others may represent and sign jointly.

The managers may also authorize employees to make and sign legally binding statements in respect of a specified group of affairs. Any limitation must be entered in the Commercial Register.

2.5.3 The supervisory board

The supervisory board controls the management of the economic association. It examines the reports, balance sheet and inventory or property to be submitted to the members' meeting and the chairman of the supervisory board then discloses the findings of such examination to the members' meeting.

Whenever it is warranted by the size of the membership, or the importance or character of the company activities, the articles of association may provide for a supervisory board. A supervisory board must be formed by the limited liability company only if
– the stock capital exceeds HUF 20 million, or
– the number of members exceeds 25, or
– the number of full-time exployees exceeds 200 persons on an annual average.
In the case of a one-man company the establishment of a supervisory board is mandatory only if the number of the annual employees exceeds 200 persons.

Pursuant to the Company Act the supervisory board consists of at least three members.

The members of the supervisory board are generally elected by the members' meeting, except for the first supervisory board, whose members are appointed in the articles of association.

The general liability rule of the Civil Code is applicable to the members of the supervisory board, namely that they are liable for any damage caused by breach of duty to the economic association, and this liability is unlimited.

The rules of incompatibility are similar to those relevant for the manager with the additional regulation that an employee of the company may not be elected to the supervisory board.

The competence of the supervisory board is different from that provided under the relevant rules in many other European countries where the supervisory board is sometimes the supreme executive body of the limited liability company. According to the Hungarian regulations it is the manager who has this competence and there is no way to empower the supervisory board with an executive-managing competence.

2.5.4 The auditor

It is mandatory to appoint an auditor
- in a one-man company
- in a limited liability company with stock capital exceeding HUF 50 million.

The auditor's tasks in limited liability companies without a supervisory board are the same as that of the supervisory board. In companies where there is a supervisory board operating it is reasonable to divide the duties.

The auditor must have passed a state examination on Hungarian accounting principals and must be registered with the Minister of Finance.

Chapter 3

The company limited by shares (Co. Ltd.): Rt

3.1 General

A public company limited by shares is referred to in Hungarian as Részvénytársaság or by its abbreviation Rt.

The provisions of the Company Act regulating the Co. Ltd. are mandatory and no departure from these regulations is permitted without explicit mention in the Act. Since the theoretical basis of the Co. Ltd. is similar to that in other European countries (and in particular the Federal Republic of Germany and Austria), only the most important special rules shall be reviewed.

3.2 The registered capital

The minimum amount of the registered capital, as determined by the Company Act, is HUF 10 million. The cash contribution may not be less than 30 per cent of the registered capital and in no event may be less than HUF 5 million.

3.3 The founders

The Company Act permits one member to establish a Co. Ltd. (a 'One-man Co. Ltd.') but only if it is founded by a state-budgeted organization or a financial institution.

The founders may be natural or legal entities.

3.4 The participation of a foreigner

A foreign natural person may be a member of a Co. Ltd., but may only acquire registered shares. In the event a foreigner inherits bearer shares, they must be converted into registered shares by the company within one year.

13

3.5 Shares

3.5.1 General

Shareholding in a Co. Ltd. is evidenced by share certificates issued by the company. The formal requirements for the shares of a Co. Ltd. are strictly determined by the Company Act and only those shares which satisfy these requirements are effectively operative as securities. Additionally, Act VI of 1990 on the Public Marketing of Securities and the Stock Exchange (hereinafter also referred to as the 'Stock Exchange Act') has created further information requirements for the issuance and marketing of shares. The Stock Exchange Act came into force 1 February 1990 and, as of the time of this publication, no commentary or legal interpretation are yet available.

3.5.2 Compulsory items on share certificate

The law provides for various compulsory items which must appear on the share certificate. These include:
- the firm name;
- the seat of the Co. Ltd.;
- the serial number;
- the face value of the share;
- a statement whether it is a bearer share or a registered share;
- the owner's name;
- the class of the share;
- the rights attached to the share;
- the date of issue;
- the amount of the registered capital;
- the number of shares at the time of issue; and
- the signature of the board of directors.

3.6 Types of shares

3.6.1 Bearer shares and registered shares

There are basically two types of shares in a Co. Ltd., namely bearer shares and shares registered in the name of the shareholder.

3.6.2 Share warrants and temporary shares

Additionally, the share warrant and the temporary share are special securities substituting for shares. Until the registration of the Co. Ltd. a certificate justifying the existing membership and material rights is given to the shareholders in the form of a share warrant. After the entry of the Co. Ltd. in the Commercial Register but before the payment of the entire registered capital, a temporary share may be issued on the paid-up registered capital. Both securities may only be registered shares.

3.6.3 Special classes of shares

The Company Act introduced several special classes of shares. These include:
- preference shares;
- depreciating shares;
- workers' shares;
- shares entitling owner to predetermined interest;
- convertible bonds; and
- preference bonds.

3.6.3.1 Preference shares

A preference share entitles the holder to a dividend from the distributable profit prior to the holders of other types of shares. It is possible, then, that the holders of non-preference shares do not receive a dividend. The rules of dividend preference are stipulated in the articles of association which may limit or exclude the voting rights attached to the preference shares.

The value of the preference shares may not exceed 50 per cent of the registered capital.

3.6.3.2 Depreciating shares

Depreciating shares pass into the ownership of some public fund or society after the lapse of a certain period as determined in the articles of association, without any legal action on the part of the holder. The beneficiary is entitled only to the sum corresponding to the face value, while the difference between the face value and the market value is due to the shareholder.

3.6.3.3 Workers' shares

The workers' shares may only be registered shares. They are transferable among the employees and pensioners of the company. There are numerous conditions for issuance of workers' shares:
- they may not be issued at the foundation, but rather only during the operation of the Co. Ltd.;
- they may be issued only from the assets of the company exceeding the registered capital;
- the registered capital must be increased;
- their value may not exceed 10 per cent of the increase in the registered capital;
- the articles of association must give authorization for their issuance.

3.6.3.4 Shares entitling owner to a predetermined interest

According to definition, the owner of 'shares entitling owner to a predetermined

interest' is entitled to the interest even if the Co. Ltd. has no profit in the given year. There are, however, limitations, namely that
- it may be paid only from the assets of the Co. Ltd. exceeding the registered capital;
- such shares may be issued only up to 10 per cent of the registered capital.
The owner is entitled to dividends as well, in addition to the predetermined interest.

3.6.3.5 Convertible bonds

A convertible bond is a security embodying a credit which must be converted into a share of the company at the request of the owner.

The owner first gives a credit to the company, and the company is then obligated to pay back both the nominal value of the bond and the indicated interest within the contractual term, unless the owner indicates that he wishes to become a member in the Co. Ltd., in which case the bond must be converted into a share.

3.6.3.6 Preference bonds

The owner of a preference bond is entitled to an option to buy new shares issued by the Co. Ltd.

3.7 Methods of founding a Co. Ltd.

The founding of a Co. Ltd. takes place in one of two ways:
- public foundation; or
- foundation in camera.

3.7.1 The public foundation

3.7.1.1 State supervisory organ

The Stock Exchange Act created a new state supervisory organ which is subordinated to the Ministry of Finance. Its function is to supervise the public issuance and marketing of securities and the legal operation of the stock exchange. For public foundations of a Co. Ltd., the Stock Exchange Act requires that the issuer make a public offer for the subscription of shares and publish an information sheet. The content of these documents must be verified by the state supervisory organ.

3.7.1.2 Draft of the deed of foundation

In a public foundation the founders issue an offer called draft of the deed of foundation. The Company Act requires that this includes the most important data of the Co. Ltd., including:
- the name, seat and scope of activities of the Co. Ltd.;

- the period of duration of the Co. Ltd., which may be perpetual;
- the amount of the registered capital;
- the number of authorized shares;
- the face value of the shares;
- the rights attaching to each class of shares;
- the address and starting and final day of share subscription;
- the privileges granted to the founders (in particular that they are entitled to appoint the members of the board of directors for the first three years);
- the nature and value of the in-kind contribution and the number of shares to be given in consideration for the intended contribution; the name and seat (or domicile) of the contributors and the name of the auditor performing the preliminary valuation;
- the procedure to be followed in case of over- and under-subscription; and
- the manner of convening statutory meetings.

Additionally, the Stock Exchange Act has substantially increased the amount of information which must be revealed. This Act requires that the following data be included in the draft beyond what is stipulated in the Company Act:

- date of foundation;
- number of employees;
- the most important personal data concerning the leading officers (e.g. age, family status, education, profession and professional experience);
- the scope of activities of the founder which must be verified by a study concerning its production activity, marketing, research and development and investment activities;
- the date of the founder's decision to issue an offer;
- the intended use of the capital acquired in issuing shares;
- serial number;
- address and starting and final date of marketing-rights of first refusal, if any;
- intended quotation on the date of issuance;
- appointment of a company (limited liability company or company limited by shares) licensed by the state supervisory organ to market shares;
- the intended interest for any interest-bearing securities;
- address(es) of corporate cashier;
- reorganization proceedings or receiverships within the preceeding three year period;
- legal entities, if any, that guaranteee fulfillment of the obligations stipulated in the securities; and
- a statement that the issuer and the marketing organ are jointly and severally liable for misleading information causing damage to the holder of the security.

The founders are bound by the contractual offer.

3.7.1.3 Shareholders' signature of subscription sheet

By signing the subscription sheet, the shareholders declare their participation in the Co. Ltd. to be founded. At least 10 per cent of the nominal value of the shares must be paid in at subscription. This rule does not apply to contributions in kind. The foundation is deemed to be frustrated if the subscriptions do not reach the amount of registered capital determined in the draft of the deed of foundation.

3.7.1.4 The statutory meeting

The following activities take place at the statutory meeting:
- statement that the registered capital has been fully subscribed and that at least 30 per cent of it has been paid in;
- drafting of the articles of association;
- election of the board of directors, the supervisory board and the auditor for the first year; and
- decisions about the affairs enumerated in the Company Act.

Resolutions may be passed at the statutory meeting provided that
- at least five subscribers are present who together have subscribed to at least one half of the registered capital; and
- the decisions are passed by a simple majority of votes, except for any deviation from the draft of the deed of foundation which is only possible with a unanimous decision.

3.7.2 Foundation in camera

Foundation in camera is a simple method of founding a Co. Ltd. for which there is no need for the release of a draft deed of foundation, the subscription of shares or the statutory meeting. The foundation may be in camera provided that the shareholders agree to buy all the shares in the proportions defined by themselves. This agreement must be included in the articles of association of the Co. Ltd. and endorsed by a lawyer or a legal adviser.

3.8 One-man Co. Ltd.

Pursuant to the relevant provisions of the Company Act, a one-man Co. Ltd. may only be founded by a state-budgeted organization or by a financial institution as the sole shareholder. During its operation, a Co. Ltd. may become a one-man company in the event that one shareholder acquires all the shares. The establishment of a one-man Co. Ltd. must be announced to the Court of Registration within 30 days of its foundation or else the shareholder bears unlimited liability for the debts of the company.

3.9 The corporate organs

The corporate organs of the Co. Ltd. are:
- the general meeting;
- the board of directors;
- the supervisory board; and
- the auditor.

3.9.1 The general meeting

The general meeting is the supreme organ of the Co. Ltd., deciding all the matters delegated to its exclusive competence by the Company Act and the articles of association. It passes resolutions generally by a simple majority of votes, but in the most important affairs by a three-fourths majority. Affairs requiring at least a three-fourths majority include:
- establishment and amendments of the articles of association;
- increase and reduction of the registered capital;
- modification of the rights attaching to the individual types of shares; and
- decisions concerning merger, dissolution, termination and conversion of company form.

3.9.2 The board of directors

The board of directors, consisting of not fewer than three but no more than eleven members, is the managing organ of the company. Its functions include directing the working organization of the Co. Ltd. and exercising the employers' rights. Beyond management, it is the task of the board to draft the balance sheet, the inventory of assets and the proposal for the distribution of profit as well as to prepare a report on the financial status and business policy of the company once a year. Furthermore, the board of directors is responsible to inform the public as to where and when the annual report will be issued by publishing this in two daily newspapers and the official paper of the Stock Exchange.

The annual report must include:
- a description of business activities of the Co. Ltd. in the preceding year;
- a report on the financial status of the Co. Ltd. in the preceding year; and
- a balance sheet.

This information must be verified by a certified public accountant and is referred to as an ordinary obligation (in that it is an annual obligation). The board of directors also has the 'non-ordinary' obligation to inform the public of circumstances which directly or indirectly affect the value of the shares, if this information has not already been published in the last annual report.

3.9.3 The supervisory board and auditor

It is mandatory to elect a supervisory board and an auditor. The supervisory board consists of at least three members. If the number of the full-time employees of a Co. Ltd. exceeds 200 on an annual average, one-third of the members of the supervisory board are elected by the employees.

3.10 Holding rules

The Company Act provides regulations for the case when the Co. Ltd. acquires an interest in another Co. Ltd. by acquiring shares, including:
- a so-called considerable interest;

- a majority interest;
- direct supervision; and
- a mutual interest.

3.10.1 Considerable interest

A considerable interest exists when a Co. Ltd. acquires more than one-fourth of the shares of another Co. Ltd. or possesses more than one-fourth of the votes of the general meeting of the other Co. Ltd., unless this interest qualifies as majority interest. In such a case the Co. Ltd. possessing the interest must inform the other Co. Ltd. thereof and make it public in the official gazette.

3.10.2 Majority interest

A majority interest exists when a Co. Ltd. has acquired shares representing more than half of the registered capital of another Co. Ltd. or is entitled to more than half of the voting rights at the general meeting of the latter. In such a case the Co. Ltd. in which an interest is being acquired (referred to as the 'controlled company') must be advised of this intention before the acquisition, and an offer must be submitted to the shareholders of the company to be controlled regarding the intended purchase of shares. This offer must include the type and number of shares to be bought, the buying price and the term during which the interested buyer is bound by his offer. This notification and offer must be made public in the official gazette.

Any shareholder of the controlled Co. Ltd. may ask the controlling company to buy his shares at a price not less than the last offer made before the controlling company acquired the majority of shares, or to pay the shareholder a predetermined dividend. This request must be submitted within 90 days from the acquisition of the majority interest under pain of forfeiture of rights.

In the case where the controlled company is forced to carry out a business policy against its own interests under the influence of the controlling company, the court may declare that the controlling company is liable for the debts of the controlled company, upon the request of creditors representing at least 20 per cent of the debts of the controlled company.

A Co. Ltd. fully- or majority-owned by a foreigner may not acquire a majority interest in another Co. Ltd.

3.10.3 Direct supervision

A Co. Ltd. is deemed directly supervised if more than three-fourths of its shares have been acquired by another Co. Ltd. In such a case the board of directors of the company exercising direct supervision is entitled to give instructions to the board of the directly supervised company. This instruction must be executed.

The directly supervising company bears unlimited liability for the debts of the directly supervised company. The fact of direct supervision must be entered into the Commercial Register and published in the official gazette. The shareholders of the directly supervised company may, within 90 days of the acquisition of the controlling interest, request the supervising company:

– to pay them a predetermined dividend;
– to purchase their shares at the value on the date that direct supervision was obtained; or
– to exchange their shares for the shares of the supervising Co. Ltd.

It is a provision safeguarding the interests of the creditors that those with not-yet-expired claims against the company under direct supervision which arose before the publication may request a security to be furnished by the supervising company within 90 days from the date of publication.

3.10.4 Mutual interest

A mutual interest exists between two Co. Ltd.'s if each of them has acquired shares of the other company representing more than one-fourth of the registered capital, or if each is entitled to more than one-fourth of the votes of the general meeeting of the other company. In such a case the above-mentioned notification obligation exists in such a way that the company, which was the first to notify the other company, may retain its already-acquired interest, while the other company is obliged to reduce its interest to one-fourth of the registered capital.

3.11 Increasing the registered capital

The Co. Ltd. may only increase its registered capital after the nominal value of all its previously issued shares have been fully paid up. The increase may be effected by issuing new shares or by changing the company's assets exceeding the registered capital into registered capital or by converting convertible bonds into shares.

In the case of an increase of registered capital by public issuance of new shares, the issuer must have been in existence for at least one year.

Chapter 4

The forms of companies with unlimited liability

Since foreign investors are predominantly interested in companies with limited liability, the forms of economic associations with unlimited liability shall be dealt with only briefly.

4.1 The unlimited partnership

4.1.1 General

The unlimited partnership is an economic association founded by natural persons and legal entities. At least one member of the unlimited partnership must be a legal entity. The Company Act has special provisions for a sub-type of the unlimited partnership – called an economic working community – whose members are exclusively natural persons.

4.1.2 Obligations of the members

In the unlimited partnership the members undertake the obligation to pursue the economic activities of the enterprise with unlimited, joint and several liability.

The members (natural persons) of both the unlimited partnership and economic working community are obliged to personally work in the enterprise. The Company Act refers to this as 'personal collaboration'. Mere financial investment does not suffice. The character and content of this obligation are not regulated by the Company Act but must be stipulated in the articles of association. Personal collaboration is considered such a fundamental obligation that any stipulation in the articles excluding it is null and void.

The members are further obligated to make available sufficient assets for starting up the economic activities of an unlimited partnership. The Company Act does not determine the maximum or minimum, nor does it regulate their character, so that the contribution may be made in cash or in kind or by supplying negotiable and valuable rights.

4.1.3 Nature of liability

4.1.3.1 Secondary liability

The new Company Act regulates the liability of the unlimited partnership in a special way: The members are not primarily liable for the company's obligations; rather the company is primarily liable with its own assets, and the members have a secondary liability, i.e. inasmuch as the company's property does not cover the claims, the members bear liability with their own property. This liability relationship is shown in the identification of the defendants in a proceeding against the unlimited partnership. In a lawsuit filed by the creditors, the company is the first defendant, while the members are the second defendants. The so-called 'several liability' rule does not prevail, as the members may be sued only if the claims of the creditors have not been completely settled from the company's property.

4.1.3.2 Internal division of liability

The company may internally regulate the liability of the members among each other and the size of their capital contribution. Generally, the responsibility for losses is proportional to the contributions, but another arrangement may also be agreed upon by the members. It is, however, forbidden to completely exclude any member from either profit or loss.

4.1.4 Remuneration to the members

As has already been mentioned, the natural persons in an unlimited partnership are obliged for personal collaboration and a remuneration is due to the members for their services. The articles of association determine the amount of this remuneration and it must be listed among the liabilities of the company in the balance sheet, thereby decreasing the tax base of the company. Consequently, it may occur that a company has no profit, but its members earn an income as remuneration for their services.

4.1.5 Representation and management

Outside management of the company, i.e. with respect to third persons, is referred to as representation in order to distinguish it from managing the internal affairs of the company which is referred to as management.

Pursuant to the Company Act each member of the company is entitled to participate in representation and management, unless the articles of association stipulate otherwise, but any limitation concerning representation is ineffective with respect to third persons.

An unlimited partnership is not obliged to establish a separate corporate organ for the purposes of representation and management, but it is not prohibited from doing so.

All the members of the unlimited partnership are entitled to decide in the matters of the company. Generally, a simple majority of votes is required.

Unanimous voting is required for amendment of the articles of association, as well as for matters not within the ordinary or normal business activities of the company.

A two-third majority of votes is required for:
– revocation of the mandate for management and entrusting another member with the management;
– revocation of the right of representation and appointment of a new representative;
– the expulsion of a member.

The articles of association may change these basic rules and stipulate unanimous voting or a qualified majority for additional matters.

4.1.6 Termination of membership

Section 46 of the Company Act regulates the termination of membership in the company by providing general grounds applicable to each form of economic association and special grounds for the various individual forms of association. The special circumstances for the termination of the membership in an unlimited partnership include:
– common agreement of the members;
– notice with immediate effect;
– ordinary notice;
– a member's violation of the law;
– a member's death or termination if it is a legal entity;
– if the continued membership is against the law.

4.2 Economic working community

4.2.1 Definition

The economic working community is an unlimited partnership whose members are exclusively natural persons. The regulations of the unlimited partnership also govern this form of association.

4.2.2 Economic working community operating under the liability of a legal entity

A related association which is also a type of unlimited partnership is the economic working community operating under the liability of a legal entity. This is an economic working community comprised exclusively of the employees and pensioners of a legal entity, and the given legal entity assumes the liability for the obligations of the company. There is an important departure from the rules concerning the unlimited partnership, namely that the liability of the members is not unlimited in this form, but it is limited to material contributions of the members and to their incomes earned in the community in the calendar year in which the given obligation has arisen. For any obligation exceeding this amount the legal entity having assumed the liability shall be liable.

4.3 Deposit partnership

The deposit partnership is also a type of unlimited partnership where the members are either full partners or so-called silent partners. The full partners bear an unlimited liability, jointly and severally with the other full partners, while the liability of the silent members is limited to their material contributions. In the Company Act there are special provisions for this form of association mainly designed to protect creditors. The silent member is, for example, neither entitled to management, nor to representation of the company; further, the name of the silent member may not appear in the firm name without his incurring liability identical with that of the full partners.

4.4 The business union

4.4.1 General

The business union is a legal entity formed exclusively by other legal entities. Its scope of activities is limited by the Company Act and it is distinguishable in that its purpose is not mainly to pursue economic activities, but rather
– to promote the efficiency of business activities of the individual entities (for example, by engaging in common market research or advertising);
– to harmonize economic activities;
– to represent the professional interests of the legal entities comprising the business union.

4.4.2 Contribution and profit

The Company Act does not prescribe a compulsory minimal material contribution for the founding members.

In addition to the ordinary activities listed in 4.4.1 above, the Company Act provides that the business union may also pursue economic activities designed to achieve common targets. This is only possible if the articles of association identify these targets and if the members make available the necessary capital. While the profit deriving from the ordinary activities is divided equally among the members, the profit deriving from the economic activities is divided among the members in proportion to their material contribution.

4.4.3 Liability

The members bear an unlimited liability for the obligations of the union. Other legal entities may join the union, subject to the relevant conditions of the articles of association. The joining member is liable also for the union's debts having arisen prior to its joining.

4.4.4 Organization and management

The Company Act regulates the organization and decision-making of the business union.

The supreme organ is the board of directors, which has exclusive competence in those matters listed in the Company Act. The director appointed by the board is entitled to the management and representation.

The board of directors may elect a supervisory board consisting of at least three members, if this is warranted by the number of the members of the union and the importance or the character of its activities.

4.5 Joint enterprise

4.5.1 Definition

As with a business union, a joint enterprise is an economic association formed exclusively by legal entities but, this form of association is founded mainly for economic activities, i.e. its purpose is principally to make profit. The parties make available the initial capital the amount of which is not determined by the Company Act. The capital may consist of cash or in kind contributions.

4.5.2 Rights and liabilities

The members of the company bear a secondary collateral liability for the debts of the company, which is a special form of unlimited liability in which the members are liable for the debts of the company insofar as the company's property does not cover the debts. In the event the assets of the company are not sufficient, the members are then liable for the debts in proportion to their material contributions.

The members share the profit of the company in proportion to their contributions, unless the articles of association provide otherwise.

No member may be excluded either from sharing profits or from bearing losses.

4.5.3 Corporate organs

The Company Act also regulates the organization of the company as follows:
– the board of directors, which is the supreme organ of the company;
– the managing board, which is not mandatory but may be established by the board of directors at their discretion;
– the director, who effects the executive duties and exercises the employer's rights over the employees of the company;
– the supervisory board, which is mandatory only if the number of full-time employees exceeds 200 persons on an annual average.

4.5.4 Withdrawal of membership

Members may withdraw from the joint enterprise. A refund of the member's proportionate interest in the enterprise, as determined by the board of directors within the terms of the articles of association, is then due to the member within three years at the latest, unless the withdrawing member transfers or assigns its membership rights and obligations to an entering member. In such a case the withdrawing member will no longer be liable for the debts of the enterprise having arisen prior to its withdrawal, while in the case of simple withdrawal the member is liable for these debts for a period of five years following its withdrawal.

Chapter 5

Activities requiring government permission

5.1 The objects clause

The objects clause of a Hungarian company must be carefully drafted. The scope of activities of a company cannot be generally described as covering 'everything that is not contrary to Hungarian legal regulations'. It is mandatory that the activities be indicated by code number according to the list published by the Central Statistical Institute.

5.2 Limitations

As a general rule any economic activity may be pursued which does not breach a legal regulation, but permission is needed for exercising certain activities. The main limitations are as follows:
- The economic association may pursue those activities reserved for the state, state organs or state-owned economic organizations provided it has at least one member authorized to do so.
- Any economic association may pursue activities requiring the license of the competent authority only if this permission has been obtained.
- Any economic association may pursue activities requiring special expertise provided there is somebody among its members or employees who can satisfy this requirement.
- Only a Co. Ltd. may pursue banking and insurance activities.
Permission must be obtained before registration of the company and the license will state the period of effectiveness.

5.3 Foreign trade

The list of the activities requiring special license from the authorities is published in the official gazette. One of them is foreign trade.

5.3.1 Announcement

Foreign trading activities may be pursued by economic organizations that have been entered into the register of the Ministry of Trade. In the case of marketing in convertible currency the registration takes place simply on the basis of an announcement by the organization, except for commodities included in the so-called export and import list of exceptions.

5.3.2 Application for foreign trading rights

In the event an organization wants a foreign trading right for goods figuring on such a list of exceptions, the procedure is more complicated and the right is granted by an order of the Ministry. The same applies when the economic organization files for export or import rights in relation to non-convertible markets.

The application to the Ministry must include the following data:
- the activities or commodities – identified by the relevant statistical number – which are the basis of the company's intended foreign trade;
- the forecasted value (expressed in hard currency) of activities or commodities for export or import;
- a statement declaring that qualified personnel is available for the company.

5.3.3 Foreign trading permission required for each business deal

Obtaining the foreign trading right does not mean that the relevant company may freely conclude contracts with foreign firms, because the Ministry of Trade also prescribes obtaining permission for each contract.

In the case of exporting, this permission is generally a formality, but it has to be obtained before concluding the deal. In the case of importing, obtaining the license is uncertain and the procedure requires 30 days. An important exception is made, however, for items on the so-called liberalized list. There is no need to obtain permission for concluding, amending or performing a contract concerning any item included in this list, if imported from a market with convertible currency. The only requirement is that the company announce its intention to enter into a contract before its conclusion. Furthermore, it is a general rule that the importing of any license, patent or know-how from a convertible market is exempt from the permission process, irrespective of the above-mentioned list of exceptions.

5.3.4 Application for permission

When a company applies for permission concerning goods included in the list of exceptions or in relation to non-convertible markets, the relevant provisions of Order 8001/1989 of the Ministry of Trade must be taken into consideration and consequently the following data have to be indicated in the application beyond those mentioned above:
- the strategy plans concerning the goods and the markets;
- the declaration of the relevant authority (Ministry or safeguarding institution) that it is not opposed to the applicant importing or exporting such goods;

- a list of the names of the qualified personnel;
- justification that the foreign trading activity will be more effectively performed by the applicant than by those companies which have the relevant concession.

5.3.5 Time frame

In practice, it appears preferable to apply for individual permission in relation to goods figuring on the list of exceptions or to non-convertible markets. Such a permission is naturally valid only for the specific case, and the application must include the details of the deal. The authority will decide upon the application within 30 days.

The time frame involved in the procedure varies depending on the manner of registration. Registration by announcement can be concluded within 30 days, while there is a delay of 60 days possible for registration by application even if the relevant decision is positive.

Chapter 6

Companies operating in duty-free zones

6.1 Definition

The Act XXIV of 1988 on Foreign Investment in Hungary (also referred to herein as the 'Foreign Investment Act') was enacted in order to promote the direct presence of foreign capital in the Hungarian economy. Toward that end the Act provides regulations concerning economic associations with foreign participation operating in duty-free zones (so-called 'off-shore companies'). A duty-free zone is deemed to be a foreign territory from the perspective of customs procedures, foreign exchange rules and, with the exceptions regulated in the law, foreign trade rules. Likewise, an off-shore company is deemed a foreign company from the aspect of these statutory rules.

It is useful to establish an off-shore company when the company
– manufactures mainly for export purposes, and
– uses a relatively large amount of goods of Hungarian origin – 'imported' from Hungary – for this manufacturing.
It is not very important for this purpose that the company market in Hungary. This may, furthermore, be difficult because of the licensing system.

6.2 Permission required

Any form of economic associations mentioned in the Company Act may be established in a duty-free zone. The joint permission of the Minister of Finance and the Minister of Trade is necessary for the establishment in a duty-free zone of an economic association with foreign participation even when the foreign firm does not have majority interest. In any case a declaration by the Minister of Finance that the land on which the company's activity will be carried out is a duty-free zone is needed. The customs procedures in such zone are included in the Joint Ordinance of the Ministers of Finance and of Trade.

A duty-free zone may be established on land owned, handled or used by a domestic legal entity with the permission of the Central Customs and Finance Guard. The consent of the Ministry of Interior, Ministry of Trade and Ministry of Traffic, Telecommunication and Building is needed for this permission.

6.3 Accounts in convertible currency

An off-shore company may conclude its affairs in the convertible currency determined in the articles of association with the exceptions enumerated below:
– all taxes and dues;
– salaries and other allowances of the employees;
– rent for office space and public utilities fees;
– retail purchases;
– construction, repair work and mounting of equipment done in the duty-free zone;
– such other necessary provisions and services that do not belong to the sphere of the off-shore company, but are necessary for the establishment and operation of the economic association.

The above-mentioned items are to be paid for in HUF, which is to be exchanged from convertible currency by a Hungarian financial institute.

The books of the off-shore company are kept in convertible currency. The currency exceeding the initial capital of the company may be kept in either a domestic or a foreign bank, while the amount of the initial capital must be kept in a domestic bank.

The off-shore company may raise loans freely either in Hungary or abroad. It may dispose freely of its currency deposited either in Hungary or abroad.

6.4 Limitations on foreign status

Although the Act declares that the duty-free zone is considered to be foreign territory from the perspective of the application of the provisions of foreign trade rules in general, this provision has certain limitations. In order to avoid the disadvantageous situation in which selling in Hungary would require an import license, the off-shore company is deemed to be a domestic company when an international treaty limits the kinds or quantity of the Hungarian exported or imported goods or includes other restrictions in this respect. The treaties concluded by Hungary with the socialist countries determine the quantity of commodities that may be marketed among these countries. All these treaties apply for off-shore companies as well.

6.5 Extension of benefits to non-duty-free zones

The Ministry of Finance may extend the benefits given to the associations in duty-free zones to associations in non-duty-free zones operating fully or partly with foreign participation, provided these companies do not pursue activities involving the transport of goods across the border of the country. It is principally advantageous for banks and financial institutions to be in such a situation.

Chapter 7

Special regulations concerning foreign participation

7.1 Limitations imposed by the Company Act

According to the Company Act:
- A foreigner may acquire only registered shares.
- A public company limited by shares which is majority- or fully-owned by foreigners may not acquire a majority interest in another public company limited by shares.

7.2 Licensing procedure

7.2.1 General

Permission is necessary for the establishment of an economic association which is fully- or majority-owned by foreigners. If the foreign participation does not exceed fifty per cent, no permission of the authorities is needed. There is one exception, namely the off-shore company, where permission is always required regardless of the percentage of the foreign participation.

7.2.2 Joint permission of Ministers of Finance and Trade

The Foreign Investment Act declares that the joint permission of the Minister of Finance and the Minister of Trade is necessary for:
- the establishment of an association which is fully- or majority-owned by foreigners;
- the transformation of an association into such a company; and
- the acquisition of a foreign majority ownership in an economic association.

The permission of the Foreign Exchange Authority is also included in this declaration. If the foreign participation does not have majority ownership, then permission for the establishment of the association or for participation therein, including the permission of the Foreign Exchange Authority, is not necessary.

Obtaining this declaration is not necessarily the end of the process; if another license is needed for the activities of the association this must, naturally, still be obtained.

7.2.3 Permission required to begin operations

Generally, according to the relevant provisions of the Company Act, a company may begin its operation from the date of signing of the articles of association, and a company is formed by virtue of its registration with a retroactive effect to the date of signing. These provisions do not, however, apply when permission is needed either because of the scope of activities or because of foreign majority ownership. In these cases a company may begin its operation only from the date of this permission. The license stipulates how long it is valid; upon expiration a new license must be obtained.

7.2.4 Permission for change in ownership

Permission is also necessary for acquiring interest in a company majority-owned by foreigners. As a result, if the foreign shareholder sells his share in a company, which is majority-owned by foreigners, permission is necessary again. This requirement is based on the fact that one critical element has changed, namely the person of the foreign member.

7.2.5 The application

7.2.5.1 Required information

The application must include:
– the names and the seat of the Hungarian and foreign members;
– the form of association, the place of its registration, the seat and the scope of activities;
– in the case of a functioning association, the amount of its assets at the time of filing the application; in the case of establishing a new company, the planned assets;
– the method of after-tax profit distribution;
– the outline of the business plan of the company, the content of which is not stipulated but must contain data which are capable of evaluation by the Minister of Finance and the Minister of Trade (including a three-year feasibility study); and
– the deed of foundation in Hungarian, or, in the case of a functioning economic association, the modification thereof.

7.2.5.2 The authorizing ministries

The application is to be addressed to the Ministry of Finance which will issue the joint decision on behalf of the Ministry of Finance and the Ministry of Trade. In the case of a rejection of the application, an explanation must be provided with the decision. If the application is not rejected within 90 days from its filing, it is deemed to be granted. If the application was not filed in the proper form or with the proper content, the applicant may be requested to remedy the error once within a 30 day period from the date of filing. The application must then be judged on its merits within 60 days from the date of remedy of the error.

7.2.5.3 The parties obligated to file

The Act enumerates the persons who must file the application:
- in case of establishment of a new company: the Hungarian founder;
- in the case of exclusive foreign ownership: the foreign party;
- in the case of the acquisition of shares by foreigners in an already-functioning association: the association itself.

In each case the application must be filed in five copies in Hungarian.

If the application is filed by the foreign party, it must indicate a domestic partner for the service of documents.

7.3 Incentives for investments by foreigners

The basic law protecting and encouraging foreign investment is the Foreign Investment Act. Together with the Company Act, it strengthens the previous benefits by providing legal guarantees for foreign investors, including:

(a) The amount due to the foreign party from an economic association's profit, or in case of the company's dissolution or in case of total or partial alienation or transfer of his share can, provided that the association possesses the amount due in HUF, be freely transferred abroad in the currency of the investment on the instruction of the foreign party. No permission is needed for this transaction.

(b) Means of production, made available by the foreign party as contribution in kind, can be imported into the country duty free.

(c) The cash contribution in a convertible currency by a foreign member of the company can be kept on the economic association's own account in the currency of contribution and can be used freely for acquisition of means of production, spare parts and equipment for permanent use necessary for production. Means of production purchased to the debit of this account can be imported into the country duty free.

(d) All losses suffered by a foreign investor due to nationalization, expropriation, or other measures having a similar effect on the ownership rights are to be compensated for at actual value without delay. Such compensation is made by the state through the state administrative organ that has taken the measure in question. In case of infringement of law, review of the state administrative organ's action can be requested from the court. The compensation must be paid in the currency of the investment.

(e) If permission is needed for the establishment of the economic association, the application must be decided upon within 90 days from the date of the filing of the application. If the authority does not reply during this period, the permission is deemed to have been granted.

(f) The economic association may enter into foreign trade, wholesale and retail trading activities under the legal provisions relevant to other domestic economic organizations.

(g) In case of a bank or financial institution founded with foreign participation, the full value of the shares must be paid up within three years, departing from the general rule providing for one year.

(h) The economic association with foreign participation may acquire ownership or other real estate rights necessary for its economic activity as defined in the articles of association.

(i) Social insurance and pension fees must be paid only for those foreign employees who wish to make use of these services.

(j) The legal provisions relevant to wage regulations, which decree the minimum and maximum wages, apply to the companies only if the foreign participation does not exceed 20 per cent or HUF 5 million.

(k) The foreigners are entitled to certain entrepreneurial profit tax allowances and further benefits (as discussed in Chapter 11) if the profits are further invested in the venture.

Other securities beyond those provided by the Company Act and the Foreign Investment Act include:

– bank guarantees furnished by commercial banks; and
– bilateral treaties concerning protection of investments. Such treaties exist, for example, between Hungary and the Federal Republic of Germany, Great Britain and Austria.

Chapter 8

The general rules of company law

8.1 Registration

8.1.1 The Court of Registration

The foundation of and the most important modifications to companies established pursuant to the Company Act must be notified to the Court of Registration. The Court of Registration will examine the application for registration within a non-litigious procedure, and if the application satisfies legal requirements, the company will be incorporated.

8.1.2 The Commercial Register

The Commercial Register is public so that anybody may look into it and make a copy of the registered data or receive an official extract.

The information to be recorded in the Commercial Register is as follows:
– the form of the company;
– the name and seat of the company;
– the data in relation to the establishment, activities, ownership and material relationships, members of the company and dissolution of the company;
– the data in connection with the representation of the company;
– all further data, rights and facts of registration as ordered by the law.

8.1.3 Constitutive effect of registration

In the case of economic associations established pursuant to the Company Act, the registration has a constitutive effect – the company is deemed to have been created by virtue of its registration in the Commercial Register, but with a retroactive effect to the date of the signing of the articles of association or adoption of the same in the case of a public company limited by shares. This means that the Company Act makes it possible for the members of a company to begin their activity from the day of the signing of the articles of association.

8.1.4 Pre-registration liability

Until the date of registration the members of a company may undertake obligations only under the common name of the company, and those persons who have performed any act in the name of the company before its registration will bear unlimited, joint and several liability for the obligations. Exclusion or limitation of this liability is ineffective as regards the company's creditors. This liability ceases if the authorized body of the company subsequently approves the contract.

8.2 The firm name

Company law mandates that the name of the company include:
– the so-called 'leading word' (which is a word chosen by the company to distinguish itself from other similar businesses);
– the field of activity in which the company is to function; and
– the legal form of the company.

8.2.1 The leading word

8.2.1.1 Definition

A trademark, a business indicator, the name of the company's members or any other word may serve as the leading word in the company name. The name of the members bearing unlimited liability may be indicated in the name of a deposit partnership and the name of the external partner may be included in the firm name only with his consent. The inclusion of the name of a member with limited liability is, on the other hand, prohibited even with his consent. According to the Company Act, an external partner will bear identical liability with the full partners when his name is included in the firm name. This means an unlimited liability.

8.2.1.2 Trademark

The Company Law prohibits the registration of a firm name which infringes upon another person's right to use that name. The rules concerning the protection of trademarks (Act IX of 1969) are applicable. Trademark protection is available to the person who has registered the trademark. Although the trademark primarily indicates the goods or services of a company, the name of the company may also be a trademark and may be entered into the Commercial Register.

8.2.1.3 Business indicator

It is more typical that the firm name includes a so-called business indicator whose main role is to distinguish the company from other similar firms. In such a case the Court of Registration will examine, on the basis of data in the Commercial Register, whether the chosen name is misleading due to its similarity to another name. The court will not examine whether the name infringes on registered trade-marks.

8.2.1.4 Name of the company's members

The names or firm names of the company's members may also be indicated in the name of the economic association instead of the leading word. A natural person may use his family name, or the name of his legal predecessor.

8.2.2 The company's field of activity

An expression referring to the field of activity of the company must be included in its firm name in order to distinguish the company, even by its name, from other firms.

The name of a company must reflect the 'actual form and activity of the company'. Words such as 'country-wide', 'Hungarian' or 'national' as well as the names of historical persons or persons having legal interest in the name, may be included in the firm name only with the consent of the competent authority or interested person. (The district council, the Minister of Justice, and the General Secretary of the Hungarian Academy of Sciences are the competent authorities when the leading word is an historical person's name, while in other cases the supervising ministry is the competent authority.)

A foreign word may be included in the firm name only if there is no Hungarian equivalent. The firm name also has to include an abbreviation in Hungarian referring to the form of the company, for example:
– Rt for a company limited by shares;
– Kft for a limited liability company.
If the firm name is indicated also in foreign languages, the Hungarian name has to be translated by the National Institution for Translators and Translations.

8.3 Competent court

The court on whose territory the seat or premises of the company is located has competence for registration.

Chapter 9

Transformation of company form

9.1 General rules

The Act XIII of 1989 on the Transformation of Economic Organizations and Economic Associations (hereinafter referred to as the 'Act on Transformation') has made it possible for state-owned companies, cooperations, holdings, and other economic organizations to be transformed into the economic associations defined in the Company Act with their entire assets and without liquidation being necessary. It is a great advantage of the regulations that the transformation (and the transfer of assets) can take place without any taxes being due. The Act on Transformation also regulates the transformation of already-existing economic associations into another form. The reason for such a conversion could be for example a change in applicable regulations or in market conditions, or the desire to establish a more effective structure, or in order to limit liability.

It is an important element of the Act on Transformation that, with few exceptions, the decision whether or not to transform is made at the sole discretion of the organization.

9.2 Conditions for transformation

9.2.1 General

In the course of the transformation there is a legal succession when the transforming economic association ceases to exist and its rights and obligations devolve upon the successor of the economic association established by it. Pursuant to the Act the steps in the transformation are as follows:
– preparation of a plan of transformation or contract of association;
– preparation of an inventory of assets;
– satisfying the rules relevant to the establishment of the given economic association.

9.2.2 Plan of transformation

9.2.2.1 Content of transformation plan

The first precondition for transformation is preparation of a transformation plan. The Act provides the following must be included in the contents:
- It has to indicate the economic purpose for the transformation.
- It has to include a declaration of the members willing to enter into the new association.
- It has to include a draft of the new company's deed of foundation (or articles of association).
- All the requirements decreed by the law for the chosen economic association must be met. For example, in the case of a transformation into a limited liability company, it has to include the amount of the stock capital, the amount of each primary stake and a proposal for the first manager.

9.2.2.2 Contract of association

When economic associations merge or disassociate, a transformation plan is not made, but rather a contract of association, the minimum content of which is also determined by the Act:
- the name and seat of the associating companies;
- the assets of the associating companies on the basis of the inventory of assets;
- the assets (stock capital, registered capital) of the new company;
- the method and date of the merger;
- the membership rights which are due to the members of the eliminated company in the new company;
- the name of the leading officials, supervisory board members and the auditor of the new company;
- the modification of the articles of association of the new company.

9.2.3 Inventory of assets

The second precondition for the transformation is the preparation of an inventory of assets. This inventory of assets is not equivalent to the amount and composition of the transforming company's assets as fixed in its books, but includes the market value of the company's assets.

Certain limitations are provided by the Act, namely:
- The inventory of assets must be controlled by the supervisory board or supervising committee, if either is operating in the organization.
- In any case the inventory of assets must be controlled by an external auditor and his opinion must be enclosed along with the inventory.
- The value of the transforming company's assets cannot be higher than that fixed by the auditor.
- The value of the reserve assets cannot be increased.

9.2.4 Satisfying the provisions of the Company Act

The third requirement for transformation is that the formal provisions of the Company Act, relevant to the given economic association, be satisfied. Due to the special method of foundation of the successor company, the Act on Transformation provides for some departures from the provisions of the Company Act, or in some cases excludes the application of certain rules of the Company Act.

9.3 Taxation

Transformation pursuant to the Act on Transformation does not create a tax obligation except in the following case: if the share of a natural person is higher in the initial capital of the transformed company than it was before the transformation, he has to pay a personal income tax on the difference. This tax is due, according to the Act, when the assets are taken out of the company, provided this part of the assets was separately recorded by the transformed company, and no bearer security has been issued on this material contribution.

9.4 Rules protecting creditors

The Act on Transformation includes certain rules for the protection of creditors. These are necessary because the Act stipulates that transformation does not cause the claims of creditors to mature; the creditors are, however, given the option of claiming a security. The creditors are made aware of the transformation in that the Act requires information concerning the transformation to be published in the official gazette twice, with a lapse of time of at least 15 days between the two publications. The creditors may claim securities from the company under transformation within 30 days commencing from the date of the second publishing.

9.5 The transformation of state companies

It is of special interest to foreign investors that the Act makes possible the transformation of the state companies into internationally-known forms of economic associations.

9.5.1 General rules

9.5.1.1 Permitted company forms

A state company may only be transformed into a limited liability company or a public company limited by shares. Financial institutions and savings banks may only be transformed into public companies limited by shares. These rules are also applicable to the transformation of companies and subsidiaries of the legal entities

45

and for state holding companies and public utility companies. The Act includes special provisions for each type of company.

9.5.1.2 State agency

In the course of transferring assets exceeding a certain stipulated value, a state agency exercises the membership rights of the Hungarian State.

Two regulations concerning the organization and operation of the state agency have recently been issued:
- Act VII of 1990 on the Establishment of the State Agency and the Regulations on Handling and Using State-owned Assets; and
- Act VIII of 1990 on Safeguarding of Assets of State-owned Companies.

Both are effective as of 1 March 1990. These regulations provide that if a state-owned company wishes to invest a certain stipulated amount of its assets in an economic organization or wishes to transform into an economic organization, the result of which is the transfer of a certain amount of its assets, the company must notify the state agency. For example, it is mandatory to notify the state agency of an in-kind contribution to an economic organization exceeding 10 per cent of the fixed assets of the company and amounting to at least HUF 20 million.

The function of the agency is primarily to ensure proper evaluation of the state-owned assets and to protect the state's ownership rights. The state agency is authorized to:
- order a new evaluation of the assets;
- order a public tender; or
- prohibit the transaction if it evidently injures the interests of Hungarian society or would result in damage to the national economy.

It is not, however, necessary to notify the state agency:
- when the state company has published the conditions of contract (including item and price) in two daily newspapers and no more favorable terms are offered to the state-owned company during the 30-day period following publication; or
- when the company has opened competitive tendering for the item and no more favorable price is offered.

9.5.2 The transformation procedure

9.5.2.1 General

The transformation procedure varies from state company to state company as far as both decision-making and the process of transformation are concerned, depending on the type of management. In this respect, there are basically two groups of companies:
- companies under direct state control, where the company's management has limited competence in decision-making; and
- companies with self-management, where the board of the company or the general meeting has wide-ranging competence.

The basic difference between the two types of companies in transformation is that:
- In the case of a company under direct state control, it is the founding state organ

46

that makes decisions about the transformation with the consent of the Minister of Finance. For a state holding the Council of Ministers' approval is also required.
- In the case of a company with self-management, on the other hand, the board of the company or the general meeting may decide about the transformation with a two-thirds majority of votes.

9.5.2.2 Companies with self-management

The Act on State Companies provides certain conditions for the transformation of companies with self-management, which are effective only if they cannot conclude a more favorable agreement with the state agency concerning the transformation. The company with self-management is obliged to submit a draft of transformation to the state agency and may conclude a separate agreement with the state agency including the method and conditions of the transformation within 60 days from receipt of the draft. This term may be extended by mutual consent. The procedure described below is only effective if no agreement is reached.

For companies with self-management the amount of the stock capital or registered capital of the new company must exceed the value of the company's assets as recorded in its books. This surplus must be covered by external capital. The Act defines the minimum amount of the external capital as 20 per cent of the company's assets or HUF 100 million. The primary stakes or shares of the economic association established in this way are divided in the following manner:
- the contribution of the external investor is due to the external investor;
- the state agency is entitled to the number of shares or quotas worth 20 per cent (or the percentage agreed upon by the company and the agency) of the transforming company's assets before the transformation as indicated in the inventory of assets;
- the local council is entitled to the number of shares or quotas worth the value of the real property as indicated in the inventory of assets;
- the economic association has the right to sell the remaining shares or quotas within a three-year period, but the owner of these shares or quotas is the state agency. In the absence of another agreement between the company and the agency, 80 per cent of the market value of the shares or quotas must be paid to the state agency, while the remaining 20 per cent is due to the economic association.

In the course of the transformation, the external investor and the representative of the state company may freely agree on the value of the company's assets, but with the restriction that the company's assets may be evaluated as less than 80 per cent of the sum indicated in the balance sheet only with the consent of the state agency.

In establishing a limited liability company or a public company limited by shares by transformation, the state agency, the local council, the external investor and the economic association itself may be the partners.

Workers' shares must be issued from the 20 per cent of the market value of the shares or quotas sold by the company according to the provisions mentioned above. Pursuant to the general rules of the Company Act the value of these shares may not exceed 10 per cent of the company's registered capital.

9.5.2.3 Companies under direct state control

When a company under direct state control is transformed, all shares and quotas are owned by the state agency which may freely market them. If a transforming company belongs to a state holding company or if it is a subsidiary company of a state legal entity, the state agency is entitled to the quotas or shares.

9.5.3 Rules pertaining to enterprises with limited liability

The Act on Transformation enumerates those rules which represent a departure or exemption from the regulations of the Company Act in the course of the transformation. Special rules pertain to limited liability companies and public companies limited by shares.

9.5.3.1 The limited liability company

The following regulations are designed to ease the liquidity problems of most limited liability companies:
- 20 per cent of the cash contributions must be paid in before the registration of the company, 30 per cent within one year and the remaining 50 per cent within 2 years from the date of registration.
- The general requirement of the Company Act concerning the minimum 70 per cent – 30 per cent split between the cash and the in-kind contributions is not applicable. The parties are free to determine the proportion of cash and in-kind contributions.

The Act on Transformation also includes some regulations more severe than those of the Company Act, namely:
- The business share may not be transferred to another member of the company until the primary stake has fully been paid in.
- It is mandatory to have a supervisory board and an auditor for any limited liability company established pursuant to the Act.

9.5.3.2 The public company limited by shares

The aim of the following rules is to make payment by the parties easier.

9.5.3.2.1 Credited temporary shares
Financial institutions and economic organizations (as defined by § 685 (c) of the Civil Code) are entitled to certain privileges in subscribing to shares in companies formed by transformation. They may subscribe to so-called credited temporary shares. The financial institutions then have to pay in only 30 per cent and economic organizations only 10 per cent of the face value of the shares subscribed to by them at the time of subscription. The balance is then due later in installments. The social security board and the insurance organizations founded by the economic organizations are also entitled to such subscriptions.

The Budapest, County, Municipal and District Councils may subscribe to credited temporary shares without any cash payment and acquire the shares free of charge.

The value of the credited temporary shares may not exceed 20 per cent of the initial capital. There is only one exception: In the case of transformation of a state company operating in the food industry, temporary shares may be issued up to 50 per cent of the registered capital.

Temporary shares also yield dividends which are used for the payment of the face value. At the time when this sum reaches the full amount of the nominal value, a share is given to the shareholder.

The balance between the amount paid at subscription and the face value of the shares is paid back in installments from these dividends.

As a consequence of the rules permitting payment in installments, the Act provides that the provisions of the Company Act, i.e. the minimum cash contribution (30 per cent) and the one-year term for the payment of the full face value of shares are not applicable to the credited temporary shares, as these rules are in contradiction with those mentioned above.

9.5.3.2.2 Capital increase

The provisions of the Company Act regulating the increase of the capital in such a way that it is possible only if the full face value of the shares have been paid in is also not applicable. According to the Act on Transformation the registered capital may be increased also in the case where a part of the existing initial capital is covered by temporary shares.

9.5.3.2.3 Conversion of creditor's claims to shares

The Act on Transformation makes it possible for creditors of the company limited by shares to convert their claims into shares without any cash payment.

9.6 The transformation of co-operatives

The Act provides detailed regulations for the transformation of co-operatives, taking into consideration the special provisions of the Act on Co-operatives.

9.7 The transformation from one form of economic associations into another

Economic associations defined under the Company Act may also be transformed into another form pursuant to the Act on Transformation. When the form of liability also changes in the course of transformation, for instance, when an unlimited or deposit partnership is transformed into a limited liability company or a public company limited by shares, the problem of creditors' protection arises. To protect the creditors' interests, the Act decrees that all members, including those who do not participate in the new company, bear an unlimited liability for five years for the debts of the unlimited or deposit partnership arising before the decision to transform.

This period is shorter only if there is a substantive legal regulation to that effect.

In the case of changing the form of an economic association, generally the rules of the Company Act relevant to the foundation of the company apply. There are, however, certain provisions departing from the Company Act in the Act on Transformation. Such exceptions include:

- In the case of transformation into a limited liability company, the provision of the Company Act concerning the minimum cash contribution (which may not be less than 30 per cent of the stock capital, but at least HUF 500,000) is not effective.
- If a public company limited by shares is transformed into a limited liability company, the bearer shares must be converted into registered shares, and the stock capital of the new company may not be less than the registered capital was.
- The provisions of the Company Act in relation to the relative proportion of cash and in-kind contribution are not applicable.
- The rules in relation to the schedule of payment of the registered capital (simultaneously with the subscription 10 per cent, another 20 per cent before registration) are also not applicable when a member of the company under transformation subscribes to shares, but only up to the amount which equals his share in the transforming company. However, if external persons subscribe to shares or the members of the old company are willing to have a larger interest in the public company limited by shares than they had in the previous company, the relevant rules of the Company Act do apply.

9.8 Merger

The Act on Transformation makes possible the merger of economic associations in the following circumstances:
- economic associations of the same form;
- an unlimited partnership with a deposit partnership;
- a limited liability company with a public company limited by shares.

The merger can be effectuated either through association or amalgamation. In case of amalgamation, one company ceases to exist and its assets pass over to the new economic association as the general successor. In the case of association, both companies cease to exist and their assets, as a whole, devolve upon the new economic association as their general successor. In both cases the conclusion of a contract of association is mandatory, and the Act mandates its minimum content.

Chapter 10

Representative offices and information and service offices

10.1 General

Permanent commercial representative offices and information and service offices can be established in Hungary by foreigners as a means of promoting their business ventures.

The governing law concerning these forms is the Ordinance of the Minister of Trade No. 3 of 1989 (II. 26.).

10.2 Permanent commercial representation

Permanent commercial representation may be carried out in two ways:
- by a foreigner commissioning a domestic economic organization to represent it in Hungary; or
- by a foreigner establishing a representative office in Hungary.

10.2.1 Through a domestic economic organization

If the commercial representation is implemented by a domestic economic organization on behalf of a foreigner, a foreign trade contract must be concluded between the organization and the foreigner.

10.2.2 By establishing an office

10.2.2.1 General

A direct commercial representative office can be established in Hungary by foreigners. It does not qualify as an economic organization, because a foreign firm may pursue economic activities only in the forms determined by the Company Act.

10.2.2.2 Registration

A direct commercial representative office is established by virtue of its entry in a register of foreign firms kept by the Ministry of Trade. It is then also entered in the Commercial Register at the Court of Registration.

The pre-conditions of registration are that:
- the foreigner have a firm or is entered in the register of companies according to its domestic law;
- the foreigner submit an application including the data required by the Ordinance.

The Ministry will inform the applicant within 30 days about the registration or rejection.

The registration may be refused or a registered firm can be removed from the register only if the activities of the foreign firm
- infringe on the Hungarian public order, or
- contradict generally accepted customs in international trading practice, or
- endanger or violate international treaties to which Hungary is a party.

Registration can also be refused if the resident country of the applicant limits or hampers the foundation or operation of Hungarian firms operating with similar goals.

10.2.2.3 Scope of activities

The scope of activities of the representative office may include:
- the preparation, negotiation, conclusion and mediation of contracts between the foreign firm and domestic foreign trading companies and private persons;
- maintaining stock on consignment;
- information and public relations activities, including exhibitions, fairs, professional lectures;
- representation of the foreigner in third countries which does not, however, free the representative from acquiring the required permission or approvals in these countries.

10.3 Information and service offices

10.3.1 Application

A foreigner may open an information and service office only with the approval of the Ministry.

The foreign firm must announce to the Ministry its intention to establish an office by submitting the data stipulated by the Ordinance of the Minister of Trade. The information is similar to that which must be provided for a direct commercial representative office and must be verified by an extract from the appropriate registry under the domestic law of the foreigner.

The application may be refused only if the activities of the foreigner:
- infringe on the public order of Hungary, or
- violate or endanger the obligations, or the fulfilment of these obligations, undertaken by Hungary in international treaties.

10.3.2 Registration

The office must also be registered into the Commercial Register within 30 days from the approval of the Ministry of Trade. This term is also valid for the representative offices. The grounds for refusal to enter or removal from the Register must be provided in the resolution of the Ministry.

10.3.3 Scope of activities

As far as the scope of activities is concerned, the main difference between a representative office and an information and service office is that the latter may not pursue commercial activities. The Ordinance gives examples of permitted activities. The office may:
– inform the Hungarian partners about the goods and services of the foreigner;
– assist in technical issues;
– perform servicing activities;
– carry out marketing activities;
– perform quality control activities; and
– provide professional consultation.

10.4 Employees

The representative offices and the information and service offices may have Hungarian and foreign employees. As far as the foreign employees are concerned, their personal data must be presented to the Ministry of Trade, and the person in question may start his activities only after the Ministry has informed the applicant of acceptance of this notice.

Chapter 11

Taxation

11.1 Introduction

This chapter reviews the rules of taxation concerning economic organizations with foreign participation and provides a brief summary of personal income tax regulations.

The taxation of the organizations outlined in this book may be divided into two groups. The first includes the taxation of the economic organizations, the second the taxation of commercial representative offices and information offices. (As already mentioned, the organizations belonging to the latter group are not economic organizations.)

It must be noted that Hungarian accounting principles are not in all respects identical with international accounting principles and the terminology is not, then, completely interchangeable.

11.2 Taxes paid by economic organizations

Payments which must be made by economic organizations include:
– entrepreneurial profit tax;
– general turnover tax;
– contribution to the central technical development fund;
– for a transformed company, a percentage payment to the state on retained business shares.

11.2.1 Entrepreneurial profit tax

11.2.1.1 General rules

The entrepreneurial profit tax is regulated by the Act IX of 1988 as modified by Act XLIV of 1989.

This tax must be paid by all taxpayers which pursue manufacturing or servicing activities for consideration in a business-like manner. The tax obligation begins on the date of signing of the articles of association, or if a special permission is needed, the date of receipt thereof, but in any case only after registration of the company. The obligation to pay this tax does not depend on whether the company has any income.

All economic organizations must register with the competent office for tax control and tax administration.

11.2.1.2 The rate of taxation

Since the reform effective 1 January 1990, the tax rate is 35 per cent on assessable income below HUF 3 million and 40 per cent on assessable income exceeding HUF 3 million.

At the taxpayer's election, losses may be carried forward into the following two financial years. No loss carry-back is permitted.

11.2.1.3 Tax allowances reducing the amount of entrepreneurial profit tax due

11.2.1.3.1 General rules
The following rules concerning tax allowances are applicable to economic associations regardless of whether there is foreign participation:
- Allowances are due to the taxpayer automatically without application.
- Tax allowances due on the basis of different regulations or titles may be used together, but only up to the total sum of the actual tax. The maximum which can be reached is a 100 per cent tax holiday.
- No tax allowance may be made use of in the following year.

11.2.1.3.2 Tax allowances due to economic associations with foreign participation
In addition to these general rules, there are special tax allowances due to economic associations with foreign participation which have also been strengthened by the Act XXIV of 1988 on Foreign Investments in Hungary.

The tax allowances due to economic associations with foreign participation may be divided into three groups.

Group 1

(a) If the foreign participation reaches 20 per cent or HUF 5 million of the initial capital, the company is entitled to a 20 per cent tax reduction of the calculated tax.
(b) If more than half of the earnings of the company originates from manufacturing products or running a hotel established by the association, and if the initial capital exceeds HUF 25 million and the foreign participation is at least 30 per cent, the company is entitled to a 60 per cent tax reduction during the first five years, and a 40 per cent tax reduction from the sixth year.
(c) If the requirements set forth in point (b) are satisfied and furthermore if the company's activity is one of the outstanding important activities included in Enclosure 5 of the Act XLIV of 1989, the company is entitled to a *100 per cent tax holiday* in the first 5 years and a 60 per cent reduction from the sixth year.

Group 2

If the conditions stated in points (b) and (c) of Group 1 exist and the foreign party uses his profit to increase the company's capital, the economic association is entitled to a tax allowance (in the form of tax retention) equal to the amount of the profit paid in to increase the capital. This tax allowance is available only on the condition that the net profit reaches the aggregate amount of the invested profit and of the tax related thereto.

Group 3

A tax allowance for a longer period or a greater tax allowance may be granted than those set forth in the Act on Entrepreneurial Profit Tax by an ordinance of the Council of Ministers for economic associations with foreign participation
– with foreign participation of at least 20 per cent or HUF 5 million of the initial assets; and
– acting in the field of banking, or
– dealing with one of the activities of outstanding importance, as indicated in the Enclosure 5 of Act XLIV of 1989.

11.2.1.4 The payment of the tax

The taxpayer itself is obligated to assess, declare and pay the taxes due. The entrepreneurial profit tax must be calculated and declared yearly and an advance payment is to be effected twice a month.

11.2.2 General turnover tax

11.2.2.1 General remarks

Economic associations pay a general turnover tax pursuant to Act XI of 1989 on General Turnover Tax. This tax serves the same function as the value added tax in Western countries.

11.2.2.2 Taxable events

The main taxable events are the marketing of products and the rendering of services as well as their export and import. There are exceptions in relation to some goods and services for which no tax is imposed at marketing, but for these products the taxpayer may not seek reimbursement for previous turnover taxes burdening the purchases (a 'pre-tax credit').

11.2.2.3 Taxable persons

The general turnover tax is paid by the natural person, legal entity or economic association without legal personality which conducts a business activity, that is markets on a regular basis in order to acquire income. Although the party engaged in the marketing is the taxpayer, it is the enduser who is actually burdened by this tax, since the seller calculates the tax into his prices.

In case of importing goods or services, the tax is to be paid by the first domestic owner or user.

11.2.2.4 The tax rate

The tax rate is 25, 15 or zero per cent of the basis of assessment. The majority of products are taxed at the rate of 25 per cent. Services of a so-called non-basic character are taxed at the rate of 15 per cent, and basic services at zero per cent. The zero per cent rate is also applicable to the exporting of goods or services. The zero per cent rate is the same as the exemption from taxes in the sense that no tax is to be paid on marketing in either case, but the difference is that in case of the zero per cent rate the taxes previously accounted may be deducted, while there is no possibility for such deduction if the given product is exempt from taxation. In the case of exporting no tax is included in the price.

There is a reduced rate prevailing in the retail trading and catering services and also if the expected income does not exceed HUF 1,000,000.00 yearly.

Finally, there are special provisions for the refund of the turnover tax, where the previously accounted tax may be reclaimed, for example, the turnover tax paid on the materials used in constructing a private home.

11.2.2.5 Basis of assessment

The basis of assessment of the general turnover tax is generally the market value of the product or service, reduced by the amount of the tax. For importing the basis of assessment is the price of the product increased by the customs duty and customs fee (if the commodity is imported from a market with convertible currency).

11.2.2.6 Contributions in kind

No general turnover tax is levied on in kind contributions.

11.2.2.7 Special rules for payment of the tax

In case of an investment by an economic association with foreign participation, 100 per cent of the general turnover tax arising in the given calendar year and previously accounted may be retained.

11.2.2.8 The character of the taxation system

Within the general turnover tax system all taxpayers pay a tax on the value added by themselves to the given product or service. The taxpayer may deduct the tax previously paid on the purchases.

This process means that the tax to be paid to the tax authorities at a given point in the marketing chain (or to be reclaimed from the tax authorities) is identical to the difference between the tax conferred onto the buyer at selling and the tax paid by the seller when purchasing. It is natural that only those who process and sell the product may deduct the tax, i.e. in the case of goods or services used for consumption, the tax previously paid may not be deducted. The amount deducted is equal to the tax indicated on the invoice.

In the case of imported goods the tax paid on the imported commodities may be deducted.

11.2.3 Contribution to central technical development fund

11.2.3.1 General

Economic associations whose yearly income exceeds HUF 25 million must contribute to the so-called central technical development fund.

This contribution is 4.5 per cent of the basis of assessment, which is equal to the tax base for the entrepreneurial profit tax.

The provisions concerning the central technical development fund are included in Act XI of 1988.

11.2.3.2 Allowances to economic associations with foreign participation

The allowances due to economic associations with foreign participation are as follows:
- If the foreign participation reaches 20 per cent or HUF 5 million of the initial capital a 20 per cent reduction on the calculated contribution is granted.
- If more than half of the income of the economic association is the result of the manufacturing of products or of running a hotel which has been established by the company and if the initial assets of the association exceed HUF 25 million and the foreign participation is at least 30 per cent, then the company is entitled to a 60 per cent reduction on the calculated contribution during the first 5 years and a 40 per cent reduction from the sixth year onwards.
- If the requirements set forth in the previous paragraph are satisfied and furthermore if the economic association's activity is in one of the fields of outstanding importance, the company receives a 100 per cent holiday in the first 5 years and a 60 per cent reduction from the sixth year onward.

11.2.4 Payment to state on retained business shares

Pursuant to Act XLIII of 1989 economic associations established according to the Transformation Act must pay a fixed percentage of its profits to the state on retained business shares.

11.2.5 The accounting system

A simple ledger system may be used if the annual income of the business does not exceed HUF 25 million and if the taxpayer is an economic association without legal personality. A simplified double entry system may be used if the annual income does not exceed HUF 250 million and the company does not belong to the above-mentioned group. A double entry system must be used if the annual income is more than HUF 250 million.

The above-mentioned categories are important not only in relation to bookkeeping, but the calculation of the basis of assessment is also different in each category.

11.3 The taxation of direct commercial representative offices and information and service offices of foreigners

11.3.1 General

The relevant ruling concerning the taxation of direct commercial representative offices and information and service offices of foreigners is the Ordinance of the Minister of Finance No. 66 of 1988 (XII. 26.). The taxpayer is the foreign company which pursues taxable activity in Hungary.

11.3.2 Taxable activity

11.3.2.1 For commercial representative offices

The taxpaying obligation starts on the day when the taxable activity of the commercial representative office begins. The domestic activity of a foreign company is deemed to be taxable if it lasts continuously for at least 3 months, or all together for 3 months within one calendar year.

However, the foreign company's activity is always taxable notwithstanding its duration, if
– the activity is based on a legal relationship with a legal entity having its seat in Hungary, or with an organization without legal personality, or with a natural person; or
– the foreign company has a representative, representative office, branch office or premises in Hungary for promoting its activity.

Notwithstanding the above, the activity is not subject to taxation if the premises are not used for performing such activities as submitting offers and concluding or preparing contracts, but rather only as a showroom or for storage.

As a consequence of the above general rules, the activities of commercial representative offices are usually taxable as the aim of their establishment is the promotion of the foreign company's commercial activities. Their typical duty is to prepare contracts and this activity is subject to taxation.

11.3.2.2 For information and service offices

The typical tasks of these offices are supplying information and showing goods. These activities are not taxable. In the case where such an office also performs servicing activities, these are not taxable when effected within the guarantee period (as they are done without consideration) but after the guarantee period such activities are subject to taxation.

11.3.3 The basis of assessment

The basis of assessment depends on the character of the foreign company maintaining the representative office. If the foreign company is a manufacturing and marketing company, then the basis of assessment is 6 per cent of the market value paid to the foreign company (i.e. the marketing organization) in the given year.

There are exceptions to this general rule:
– The commission paid on Hungarian exports has to be deducted from this base of assessment.
– If the deal is the result of the Hungarian representative's participation in a third country (except for Hungarian exports), the basis of assessment is 5 per cent of the income derived from the deal.

In the case where the foreign economic association is not a manufacturing company but only pursuing commercial agency activities and if none of the companies in the association which are active in production owns more than 15 per cent, then the taxable profit is the same percentage of the market value of the goods and services exported into Hungary by the represented companies, as the firm is entitled to for its activities from the company that has commissioned it. In case of marketing their own goods, the basis of assessment is the gross profit earned in Hungary through marketing.

11.3.4 Reducing the basis of assessment

If the foreign economic association has a representative office in Hungary, the basis of assessment may be diminished by 10 per cent.

11.3.5 The tax rate

The tax rate is 40 per cent of the basis of assessment according to the above-mentioned rules.

11.3.6 Recording obligation

Enclosure 1 of the above-mentioned Ordinance includes a questionnaire to be filled out by the foreign company. For the taxable activities, the market value of the imported goods and services must be indicated for each contract in Forint and in convertible currency. The Forint amounts must be determined according to the relevant foreign exchange rate of the Hungarian National Bank issued on the last day of the given year.

11.3.7 Declaration obligation

Both the beginning and the completion of the taxable activity must be declared to the tax office within 15 days.

The assets of the foreign company in Hungary may be taken out of the country only if the tax office has confirmed the fulfillment of tax obligations.

11.4 Personal income tax

11.4.1 General

As a general rule, natural persons earning personal income in Hungary must pay personal income tax unless international treaties provide otherwise. Hungary is party to double taxation treaties with Austria, Great Britain, Federal Republic of Germany, The Netherlands, India, Japan, Spain, Switzerland and Yugoslavia.

The Act XLV of 1989 includes the provisions regulating personal income tax. This Act entered into force on 1 January 1990.

11.4.2 Taxable income

Pursuant to this Act personal income tax is to be paid on:
– income deriving from Hungary;
– income deriving from abroad, if the person is resident in Hungary.
The Act provides that income deriving from Hungary includes also income deriving from a duty-free zone, as well as all income deriving from a domestic labor relationship, domestic activity, domestic marketing and from any asset with a real value present in Hungary. There is only one exception, namely that the income of an employee of an economic association with foreign participation paid by the foreign member of that economic association is income deriving from abroad, provided this employee is not a resident of Hungary.

The Act enumerates 48 exceptions to taxable income (including, for example, maternity benefits, aid to orphans, family allowances and health and social services actually provided).

11.4.3 Economic associations with foreign participation

The provisions of the Act of interest to the members or employees of an economic association with foreign participation include:
– 55 per cent of the wages paid to a non-resident employee of
    (1) an economic association with foreign participation
    (2) a company having its seat abroad but performing activities in Hungary
    (3) a foreign company without legal personality
    is deemed to be income. The income includes the rent of an apartment received as a benefit or any money received for rent.
– The income received by a member of an economic association from the taxed profit of the company is deemed to be income deriving from securities and as such is taxed at a rate of 20 per cent.
– The tax rate of the income deriving from bonds, deposits in a savings bank and shares is also 20 per cent.
– The tax rate is 20 per cent on the income deriving from abroad, provided that the income-producing activities are actually carried out abroad. In such cases the basis of assessment may be decreased by the income tax paid abroad. These provisions prevail unless international treaties provide otherwise.

11.4.4 Tax rates

The following general tax rates are applicable for personal income received after 1 January 1990.

HUF	0	–	55,000	0%
HUF	55,001	–	90,000	15%
HUF	90,001	–	300,000	30%
HUF	300,001	–	500,000	40%
HUF	500,001 and above			50%

11.4.5 Exceptions concerning basis of assessment and tax rate

The general rule is that 100 per cent of personal income is subject to taxation at the rates listed above.

The Act defines exceptions as far as the basis of assessment and the tax rate are concerned. These exceptions concern income deriving from:
(a) labor relationship,
(b) patent,
(c) scientific and artistic activities,
(d) farming,
(e) economic association,
(f) individual enterprise,
(g) selling real estate or a movable and valuable right,
(h) making use of certain real estate,
(i) securities and deposits in a savings bank,
(j) labor contracts abroad.

11.4.6 Deductions

The amounts paid for acquiring shares, business shares and other securities defined in the Act may be deducted from the total income, provided these are in the possession of the taxpayer on the last day of the year. However, this deduction cannot exceed 30 per cent of the total income deriving from Hungary from a foreign labor relationship or otherwise from abroad.

The tax has to be paid on this deducted amount only if the bond has been sold or if the company ceases to exist without a successor. If the assignment or the dissolution takes place within two years reckoned from the last day of the year when the security had been acquired, the tax previously saved must be paid back (plus an interest fee of 2 per cent per month, but not exceeding 30 per cent). If this condition occurs after two years, the deducted amount has to be added to the income of the person in the year when the obligation arises (i.e. when the bond is sold).

11.4.7 New tax aspects

11.4.7.1 Accounting of expenditures

Departing from previous legislation, the new Act provides a wide possibility for the accounting of expenditures. Depreciation and the general turnover tax are items, among others, which may be accounted as expenditures. Enclosure 1 of the Act includes detailed rules on this topic.

11.4.7.2 Adjourned tax payment

There is a new element in the Act, namely the possibility for adjourned (or delayed) tax payment. The relevant rules apply for securities acquired free of charge (such as worker's shares), except for the securities of co-operatives. This adjourned tax payment has been introduced because natural persons may not have the money to pay the tax when acquiring the security; therefore, the tax obligation is postponed until the security is sold. The amount of the adjourned tax must be indicated annually in the tax return.

11.4.7.3 The taxpayer

Pursuant to the Act, all items of income in the given year must be added together except for those items determined by the Act. The natural person is obligated to himself calculate the tax due, to declare this in his tax return, and, naturally, to pay the tax.

Tax-free income and that deriving from deposits in a savings bank and from securities, as well as income in nominal amounts, need not be indicated in the tax return.

In the case when all income derives from one labor contract or membership, the tax will be defined, deducted and paid by the employer; in all other cases, it is the employee's obligation.

Chapter 12

Acquisition of real estate by foreigners

Although the Hungarian legal provisions are not entirely consistent, it does appear that an economic association with foreign participation is entitled to acquire real estate in Hungary.

Section 19 of the Act of Foreign Investment provides that a company with foreign participation is entitled to acquire real estate or rights in real estate which are required for its economic activities as defined in its articles of association (or company statutes).

This position is also verified by a recent ordinance of the Ministry of Finance issued in 1990 (No. 5) which provides that no permission from the foreign exchange authorities is necessary if a joint venture fully-owned by foreigners, having its seat in Hungary, wishes to construct a building or acquire real estate rights which are necessary for its business activities as defined in the articles of association. The same rule is then made applicable to other economic associations having foreign participation which wish to acquire property rights in real estate.

A contrary position is, however, provided by an Ordinance of the Ministry's Council issued 12 December 1989 (No. 145). For the purposes of this ordinance, a foreigner is defined as including a legal entity with foreign participation having its situs in Hungary. According to the Ordinance a foreigner must apply for permission from the Center of Financial Affairs for the acquisition of real estate by way of purchase, exchange or donation. According to a recent decision of the Hungarian constitutional Court, Ordinance No. 145 will be taken out of force effective 30 September 1990.

Chapter 13

Dispute resolution

13.1 General

All disputes arising out of a contractual relation between a foreign party and a Hungarian party may – subject to agreement – be brought in the competent Hungarian state court or in Hungarian arbitration court. The basis of the freedom of parties to agree rests on Section 62 of the Hungarian Code on Private International Law which provides:

> 'In case of a legal dispute arising in contracts of international economic relations the parties may, by written stipulation, determine the jurisdiction of a foreign or Hungarian, ordinary or arbitration court.'

Hungarian law is very liberal concerning the choice of law for the settlement of disputes and for the law applicable to the contract. The parties are free to chose the applicable law in international contracts and when the contract is silent on applicable law, the Hungarian conflict of laws rules (as defined in the Code on Private International Law) are applicable.

13.2 Arbitration

13.2.1 Hungarian regulations

Arbitration is increasingly resorted to in Hungary as a method of settling disputes arising in the context of international commercial transactions.

Hungary does not yet have a statute dealing exclusively with commercial arbitration although some circles expect the passing of an arbitration act in Hungary in 1990. The main source of law in this context is Chapter 24 of the Code of Civil Procedure and the new rules of procedure for the Court of Arbitration of the Hungarian Chamber of Commerce. Chapter 24 allows for both *ad hoc* arbitration and arbitration before the Court of Arbitration of the Hungarian Chamber of Commerce.

13.2.2 Ad hoc arbitration

Ad hoc arbitration may be agreed upon between a Hungarian economic organization and a foreign party, or between foreign parties. Parties are in no way restricted as to the choice of arbitrators or the rules of procedure. Parties may agree to the rules in their contract but frequently agree to arbitrate under the International Chamber of Commerce, Paris (ICC) rules or the UNCITRAL rules.

13.2.3 The Court of Arbitration of the Hungarian Chamber of Commerce

The Court of Arbitration of the Hungarian Chamber of Commerce in Budapest has its own rules of procedure effective as of 1 September 1989, which are quite similar to the UNCITRAL rules. The hearings are not public and the decisions are treated confidentially. The language of the proceedings may be chosen by the parties; if no choice is made, then the language of the contract prevails. Of particular interest to foreign investors is that the new rules of procedure make possible the nomination of non-Hungarian arbitrators. The Court of Arbitration of the Hungarian Chamber of Commerce has a panel of arbitrators which are available; the parties may, however, freely appoint arbitrators who are not entered on the panel. If the two arbitrators chosen cannot agree on the presiding arbitrator, he will be appointed by the arbitration court from this panel of arbitrators.

13.2.4 Bilateral agreement

Hungary has entered into a number of bilateral arbitration agreements with standing arbitration courts in other countries. The Cooperation Agreement between the Austrian Federal Economic Chamber, Vienna and the Hungarian Chamber of Commerce, Budapest signed on 6 October 1982 is a well-known example. It recommends the following arbitration clause:

> 'Any disputes arising from this contract, including those disputes relating to the validity, interpretation or termination of the contract shall be exclusively and finally settled by an arbitral tribunal formed and administered in conformity with Articles 2 and 3 of the Arbitral Agreement between the Austrian Federal Economic Chamber, Vienna and the Hungarian Chamber of Commerce, Budapest.'

Article 2 of this Cooperation Agreement provides that the UNCITRAL Arbitration Rules (1977 version) as modified by the Agreement are applicable. These modifications concern the submission of the notice of arbitration (Article 3), the statement of claim (Article 18) and the statement of defense (Article 19). These are to be submitted to the Secretariat of the Arbitral Tribunal of the contracting party whose President is the appointing authority in conformity with paragraphs a and b of Article 2:
- For disputes between parties having their place of business in the territory of the Republic of Austria and parties having their place of business in the territory of the Hungarian People's Republic the appointing authority shall be either the

President of the Austrian Federal Economic Chamber of Commerce, Vienna, if the claimant (respectively the counter-respondent) has its place of business in the territory of the Hungarian People's Republic or the President of the Hungarian Chamber of Commerce, Budapest if the claimant (respectively the counter-respondent) has its place of business in the territory of the Republic of Austria;

– For disputes between parties having their place of business in the territory of the Republic of Austria or in the Hungarian People's Republic and parties having their place of business in the territory of a third country the appointing authority shall be either the President of the Federal Economic Chamber, Vienna, if a party has its place of business in the territory of the Hungarian People's Republic or the President of the Hungarian Chamber of Commerce, Budapest, if a party has its place of business in the territory in the Republic of Austria.

The Cooperation Agreement also provides for the establishment of a common list of arbitrators and a common schedule of the arbitrators' fees and administrative charges.

13.2.5 Enforcement of an arbitral award

Once the parties have agreed to resort to arbitration no other judicial procedure is admissible.

Arbitral awards passed by Hungarian arbitral courts are enforceable in the same way as judgments of ordinary Hungarian courts (Law Decree No. 18 of 1979). As a rule, all arbitral awards are final and there is no possibility of appeal to the ordinary courts. The exceptions are very similar to the grounds for non-enforcement of Arbitral awards under the New York Convention. An award can be set aside by the Municipal Court if the Arbitral Court did not have jurisdiction or exceeded its competence, if a party was denied the opportunity to be heard or if the award violates Hungarian public policy. The writ of execution is to be applied for at the Budapest Metropolitan Court which examines whether the conditions for execution exist or not.

Hungary is a member of the 1958 New York Convention on the Recognition and Enforcement of Arbitral Awards with two standard reservations. First, Hungary will apply the Convention of the recognition and enforcement of awards made only in the territory of another contracting state. Second, Hungary will apply the Convention only to differences arising out of a legal relationship, whether contractual or not, which are considered as commercial under Hungarian national law.

Hungary, furthermore, is a signatory of the 1961 European Convention on Arbitration and participates in the International Center for the Settlement of Investment Disputes (ICSID).

Hungary is also party to the Convention of Moscow concluded in 1972 on the Settlement by Arbitration of Civil Law Disputes which provides that disputes shall be settled by the Courts of Arbitration attached to the Chamber of Commerce of the COMECON countries. As other COMECON countries Hungary has a long tradition of arbitration as a method of dispute settlement.

Index of Statutes

1. Act VI of 1988 on Economic Associations
2. Act XXIV of 1988 on Foreign Investments in Hungary
3. Act XIII of 1989 on Transformation of Economic Organizations and Economic Associations
4. Ordinance of the Minister of Trade No. 3 of 1989 (II. 26)
5. Act XLIV of 1989 on Entrepreneurial Profit Tax
6. Act XI of 1989 on General Turnover Tax
7. Act XLIII of 1989
8. Act XLV of 1989 on Personal Income Tax
9. Regulation on Private Entrepreneurs
10. Act VI of 1990 on the Public Marketing of Securities and the Stock Exchange
11. Act VII of 1990 on the Establishment of the State Agency and Regulations on Handling and Using State-owned Assets
12. Act VIII of 1990 on the Safeguarding of Assets of State-owned Companies
13. Act IX of 1969 on Trademarks
14. Ordinance of the Minister of Finance No. 66 of 1988
15. Act on Co-operatives

Enclosures

This translation of Hungarian Rules of Law in Force prepared by Ötlet Ltd. (postal address: Gyáli ut 3/b, H-1986 Budapest) is regularly published in two weeks intervals.

1. Act VI of 1988 on Economic Associations

It is the purpose of the present Act to improve, by creating up-to-date legal frames, the income-earning capacity of the national economy, the development of a market-type production-and-distribution cooperation, to promote the flow of capital as well as the direct participation of foreign working capital in the Hungarian economy. This Law shall further be the more efficient utilisation of the social, and in particular, that of the State property and capital. By eliminating the impediments preventing the economic and business organizations from cooperating with citizens, it wishes to enable the use of individual savings for public purposes and intends to open wide and safe opportunities for their interests. The activities of business societies, associations, companies, and ventures may not restrict competition nor organize monopolies and may not infringe neither their reciprocal entrepreneurial nor the public interest.

Moved by the above considerations, the Parliament of Hungary has enacted the following Law on business societies, associations, ventures and companies:

Introductory provisions

Chapter I. General provisions

para. 1

(1) The present Law regulates the foundation of business societies, associations and companies (ventures), their organizations, the functioning of their bodies, their rights, liabilities and responsibilities, as well as the termination of societies, associations, and companies (ventures).

(2) The business societies, associations, companies, and ventures may, in their own name, acquire rights and enter commitments or liabilities; in particular, they

73

may acquire property, conclude contracts, may sue other parties before courts, and may be subjects of lawsuits.

para. 2

(1) Business societies, associations, companies, and ventures may be established solely in the manners and forms this Law provides.

(2) Business associations not qualifying as legal entities are: the unlimited partnership and the deposit partnership. Business societies, associations, companies, and ventures possessing a legal entity are: the association, the joint venture, the limited liability company and the company limited by shares.

para. 3

The scope of this Law does not include cooperative societies, specialized groups (teams), water management associations, working communities (workteams) having legal entity, social associations, as well as other personal unions of natural persons of purposes other than business activities; special statutory rules shall apply to all the above said societies, associations etc. The provisions of the Civil Code shall govern the civil-law association.

para. 4

(1) Business societies, associations, companies, and ventures except for those regulated by the present Law – may be founded by the State, by legal entities, by business associations having no legal entity as well as by natural persons (both nationals and aliens) for carrying on business-like, joint business activities or for promoting such activities; the said persons and legal entities may join an acting economic association as members.

(2) Inasmuch as a certain activity is reserved by a Law, law-decree or decree of the Council of Ministers for the State, a body of the State or a State-owned management or business organ, the business society, or association may pursue such an activity only if at least one of its members is entitled to do so.

(3) A business society, association, company or venture may carry on banking and insurance activities solely if it is organized as a company limited by shares.

(4) For the purposes of the present Law, the term 'natural person' shall mean any person regardless of his/her citizenship; and an alien (foreigner) is a natural person or legal entity whom (which) the statutory rules relating to foreign exchange management declare a foreigner.

para. 5

Unless a Law provides otherwise: at least two members are necessary for the foundation of a business society, association, company, venture.

74

para. 6

(1) A natural person may be a member with unlimited liability solely in a single business society, association, company or venture.

(2) A civil-law association may not be a member of a business society, association, company or venture and may not be the founder of a company limited by shares.

(3) An unlimited partnership or a deposit partnership may not be a member with unlimited liability or another similar association.

(4) Solely legal entities may be members of a union or joint venture.

para. 7

(1) Foreigners (aliens) may participate as founders of or members to a business society, association, company or venture only if they control a firm (corporation) under their own national laws or if they have been entered, according to their national laws, in a company (or other business) register. Any foreign natural person or legal entity may be a shareholder.

(para. 7(1) taken out of force as of 1 April 1990)

(2) Conditions as to participation of foreigners differing from this Law may be stipulated by international agreement.

para. 8

(1) A jointly signed licence by the Minister of Finance and the Minister of Trade is necessary for the foundation of a business society, association, company or venture with a foreign majority or fully foreign ownership, for converting a legal entity into such a company or for the acquisition of a majority foreign interest in the society, association, company or venture. The said licence includes the permit by the foreign exchange authority. If the corresponding application has not been rejected within 90 days from filing, the licence should be considered as granted.

(2) If the foreign participation is lower than indent (1) stipulates, neither a licence by the foreign exchange authority nor any other permit will be necessary for the foundation of a business society, association, company, venture or for the participation in same.

para. 9

(1) The foreigners' interest (stake) in a business society, association, company or venture enjoys full protection and safety.

(2) The part due to the foreigner from the profit of the company, as well as the sum due to the foreigner in case of the liquidation of the society, association, company or venture or the sum obtained upon the sale in full or part of the foreigner's share, shall be freely transferable abroad, without any permit by the foreign exchange authority, subject to that the society, association, company or venture possesses, in terms of money, the sum covering the transfer of foreign exchange in

question; the transfer is to be effected according to the foreigner's relevant instructions and in the invested currency.

(3) The special benefits, allowances and particular business terms favouring foreigners will be determined by a separate Law.

para. 10

(1) A business society, association, company or venture composed of solely natural persons as members may not employ more than five hundred workers/emloyees.

(2) The provision of indent (1) shall not apply to business societies, associations, companies and ventures owned in full or majority by foreigners.

(*para. 10(1) and (2) taken out of force as of 1 April 1990*)

para. 11

(1) The Court of Registration shall exercise the legal supervision of business societies, associations, companies and ventures.

(2) In the framework of the legal supervision, the Court of Registration will check whether the deed of association (articles of associations), as well as the other instruments relating to the organization and operation of the company are in conformity with the statutory rules; further whether the decisions of the bodies of the association do not infringe the rules governing the organization and operation of such associations, or the deed of association (article of association), as well as the contents of the said other instruments.

(3) The legal supervision does not encompass matters which come within the purview of other court or public administrative proceedings.

(4) The proceedings of the Court of Registration regarding business societies, associations, companies and ventures shall be applied by jointly considering the rules relating to the registration of the firms by the court and the complementary provisions contained in the present Law.

para. 12

Concerning Trade Union rights, the Labour Code, respectively the provisions of the statutory rules enacted based on the said code shall govern the labour relations of business societies, associations, companies, and ventures.

para. 13

(1) If the number of full-time employees, workers, exceeds annually the average of 200, the workers and employees of every joint venture, limited liability company and companies limited by shares shall participate, if the supervision of operation of the venture, i.e. company by participation, in the Supervisory Board.

(2) In the cases which indent (1) defines, the workers, employees shall elect one third of the members of the Supervisory Board from among themselves. The said

election shall take place at the next meeting of the Board of Directors, the Meeting of Members or of the General Assembly; this rule shall be applicable according to the meaning also in cases when the number of full-time employees or workers drops below 200.

para. 14

No bonds or securities may be issued to certify membership rights, except for the case of a company limited by shares. Any bond or security issued in spite of this prohibition shall be considered to be null and void and the persons or organizations issuing such illegal bonds or securities shall be jointly and severally liable for any damage arising therefrom.

para. 15

All facts and data relating to the business societies, associations, and ventures are public according to the statutory provisions of the present Law and the rules on the registration of firms by the court.

para. 16

(1) All statements and communications the present Law specifies shall be served to the addressee in written form or in any other way that can be proved.

(2) If the document has been mailed with the provision 'return receipt requested' it is deemed to have arrived on the date indicated on the return receipt. Failing a return receipt, it is deemed to have arrived to the inland addressee on the fifth day after mailing – unless the contrary is proven.

(3) If this Law does not define a term for making a statement or for performing a certain action, any such statement or action shall be made, i.e. carried out without delay.

para. 17

The provisions of the Civil Code shall apply to the property and personal relations of the business societies, associations, companies and/or ventures and their members, unless the present Law has regulated them.

para. 18

To legal disputes relating to the deed of association, the proceedings of the Permanent Arbitration Court, attached to the Hungarian Chamber of Commerce shall apply, provided the parties have so stipulated in the deed (articles) of association.

Chapter II. Common rules and regulations concerning all business societies, associations, companies and ventures.

Foundation of a business society, association, company or venture

para. 19

(1) Foundation of the business society, association, company or venture requires the existence of a deed of association (in case of a company limited by shares: Memorandum or Articles of Association).

(2) The deed of association shall be incorporated in a deed to be signed by all members and endorsed by a barrister or company attorney. This rule shall also apply to any amendment of the deed.

(3) The necessity of endorsement as per indent (2) shall also apply to companies limited by shares.

para. 20

The members or parties are free to determine the contents of the deed of association – within the limits set by the present Law and other statutory rules. In case of a consensus, they may depart from the provisions of the Law relating to the deed of association, except if the present Law prohibits such a departure.

para. 21

(1) The deed of association shall determine the following:
(a) the name and seat of the company,
(b) the members, partners by their names (name of firms) and domiciles (seats),
(c) the sphere of activity of the company,
(d) the size of the company's assets, the date and manner when such assets must be made available,
(e) all other details by the present Law compulsorily specifies for the given form of association,

(2) If any of the conditions listed in indent (1) is missing, the deed of association shall be considered to be null and void.

(3) Should the deed of association fail to make a provision concerning the duration (time) of the business society, association, company or venture it is deemed to have been formed for an indefinite period.

para. 22

(1) The assets of the business society, association, company or venture shall be made available by the members who will jointly share the profit, resp. the increment of the asset (hereinafter: profit) and jointly bear the losses, resp. the decrease in the asset (hereinafter: loss) in the manner as the present Law determines.

(2) Upon foundation, the assets of the business society, association, company or venture consist of the money deposits (contributions in cash) of the members as well as of the non-monetary deposits (contributions) made available by them. The non-monetary contribution may consist of any negotiable thing having the value of an asset, intellectual creation or valuable right (title).

(3) A member making a non-monetary contribution shall be liable for five years from the date of such contribution to the business society, association, company or venture that the value of his contribution has been equal, at the time of transferring it, to the value indicated in the deed of association.

para. 23

(1) The Court of Registration must be notified of the foundation of the business society, association, company or venture within thirty days from the approval of the deed of association, resp. of the adoption of the articles of association, for registration and publishing.

(2) The notification filed with the Court of Registration shall contain all data the statutory rules on the registration of firms by the Court specify. The notification must be accompanied by the documents mentioned in the said statutory rules.

(3) The Court of Registration must be equally notified of any change in the registered data within thirty days of such change.

para. 24

(1) The company is deemed to have been founded by virtue of its registration in the Trade Register – with retroactive effect to the date of the conclusion of the deed of association, resp. the adoption of the articles of association in the case of a company limited by shares. Registration may not be denied except in case of infringement of law.

(2) In fact of registration, the data so registered including any change of the latter are published in the official gazette – unless the present Law provides otherwise.

para. 25

(1) Persons who have performed any act in the name of the company before its registration, shall bear unlimited, joint and several liability for the obligations they have entered into on behalf of the common (firm) name. Any exclusion or limitation of this liability shall be ineffective in respect of the business society's, associations', company's or ventures' creditors.

(2) The liability for obligations entered into on behalf of the business society, association, company or venture prior to its registration – as defined in indent (1) above – shall cease if the body of the business society, association, company or venture authorized thereto approves the contract subsequently.

(3) If the business society, association, company or venture commences its activities before registration, it may not plead the lack of registration as exemption in respect of third parties.

para. 26

If the Court of Registration has denied registration of the business society, association, company or venture, the firm's activity must be terminated upon receipt of such a final decision. During the period from the conclusion of the deed of association until terminating the activity, the rules on the Civil Code associations shall govern – according to the meaning – the legal relations of the parties among each other and with any third party, provided that the conditions thereto exist and the parties have not otherwise decided.

para. 27

Following the registration nobody may claim that the deed of association is null and void, on grounds of error, fraud or duress (Civil Code, para. 210) arisen when adopting the deed of association. This provision shall apply – corresponding – also to any amendment of the deed.

Executive officers, members of the Supervisory Board, auditors

para. 28

Executive officers are: in case of a union and a joint venture: the director; in case of a limited liability company: the managing directors; in case of a company limited by shares: the members of the board of directors.

para. 29

(1) No one may be an executive officer of a company who has been sentenced, with final effect, for a crime, to an executable loss of liberty (imprisonment) as long as he has not been absolved from the prejudicial consequences of the criminal sentence.

(2) No one who has been barred from some occupation may be an executive officer – during the effect of the sentence – of a business society, association, company or venture which carries on the activity the sentence has indicated.

(3) The provisions of indents (1) and (2) above shall apply to members of the Supervisory Board and auditors as well.

para. 30

The executive officers, the members of the Supervisory Board and the auditors shall be appointed for a definite period of not more than five years; they may be re-elected and re-called at any time.

para. 31

(1) A person may be an executive officer in up to but not more than two business societies, associations, companies or ventures.

(2) Neither executive officers of a business society, association, company or venture nor their close relatives (cf. Civil Code, para. 685, point b.) are eligible as members of the Supervisory Board.

(3) One person may not simultaneously be elected or appointed to as member

of the Supervisory Board of more than five business societies, associations, companies or ventures. The member shall inform the interested business societies, associations, companies or ventures of any multiple election (appointment).

para. 32

(1) Executive officers, members of the Supervisory Board and auditors are held to act with the care generally expected of persons filling such offices. They are liable for any damage caused by breach of duty to the business society, association, company or venture, according to the general rules of the Civil Code. This rule applies to them if they are employed by the business society, association, company or venture.

(2) The employer may not instruct an executive officer, a member of the Supervisory Board or an auditor as long as they carry out their duties in their afore-mentioned capacities.

(3) In limited liability companies and companies limited by shares, the liability of the executive officers as indent (1) above defines, is joint and several. No liability shall be borne by an executive officer who has protested against a decision or a measure, provided he has notified the Supervisory Board or, in the absence of such board, the meeting of members (general assembly) of his objection.

para. 33

Executive officers, members of the Supervisory Board and auditors must safeguard their information on the business affairs of the business society, association, company or venture as a business secret.

para. 34

(1) The company shall file the names, addresses of members of the Supervisory Board and auditors, as well as the changes ensuing in their person, with the Court of Registration, for the purpose of entry and publishing.

(2) The Supervisory Board defines its own rules of proceeding which have subsequently to be approved by the supreme body of the business society, association, company or venture.

para. 35

(1) The members of the Supervisory Board shall elect a chairman from among themselves. The chairman must convoke the supreme body of the business society, association, company or venture, whenever the number of members of the Supervisory Board has dropped below three.

(2) Meetings of the Supervisory Board are convoked by the Chairman. Convocation may be requested from the Chairman at any time by any two members, by indicating the reason and purpose thereof; if the Chairman fails to convoke the meeting of the Supervisory Board within eight days, the said two members are entitled to convoke it.

(3) The meeting of the Supervisory Board has a quorum if two-thirds of its members, but at least three members are present. Decisions are made by the simple majority of votes.

para. 36

(1) The Supervisory Board supervises the management of the business society, association, company or venture. In the framework of such supervision it may request all the different executive leading officers of the business society, association, company or venture to submit reports or information; it may examine the books and other documents of the business society, association, company or venture or entrust an expert with such an examination.

(2) The Supervisory Board shall have to examine all reports of major significance submitted to the supreme body of the business society, association, company or venture, and further the balance-sheet and the inventory of property. The Chairman shall have to expound on the findings of such examination; in lack of such a report a valid decision may not be taken on the said reports, the balance-sheet and the distribution of profits.

para. 37

The executive officers of the business society, association, company or venture and the members of the Supervisory Board may receive a remuneration to be determined by the body of the business society, association, company or venture designated by the present Law.

para. 38

(1) The appointment of an executive officer and membership in the Supervisory Board lose its validity and effect in the following cases:
(a) upon expiry of the term of the mandate;
(b) by revocation;
(c) by waiving the mandate on behalf of the officer or member;
(d) upon the death of the officer or member;
(e) upon disqualification ensuing by causes which the present Law regulates.

(2) The provisions of indent (1) shall apply to the auditor with the difference whereby the mandate shall cease upon giving notice to him or upon his revocation or waiving his mandate.

(3) Membership to the Supervisory Board furthermore ceases when the labour relationship (employment) of a member, the workers or employees have elected, terminates.

para. 39

(1) The deed of association may provide that the auditor should carry out supervision of the management instead of along with the Supervisory Board.

(2) A company limited by shares shall have to compulsorily elect an auditor

over and above the Supervisory Board, and the same provision shall hold for a one-man venture and a limited liability company disposing of a primary capital exceeding 50 million Forint,

para. 40

(1) A person recorded in the register of chartered accountants can be elected to be an auditor.

(2) Founders members, share-holders, executive officers, members of the Supervisory Board and any close relation to the above said persons ((see point b) of para. 585 of the Civil Code) may not be the auditor; neither can an auditor be a person the business society, association, company or venture has employed, for a period of 3 years after terminating his employment.

para. 41

(1) The auditor may inspect and scrutinize the books of the business society, association, company or venture, may request information from the executive officers and the workers/employees of the business society, association, company or venture, and may examine the cash, the stock of bonds and shares as well as goods, contracts and banking accounts of the business society, association, company and venture. He may be present at the meetings or sessions of the supreme body and the Supervisory Board of the business society, association, company and venture and shall have to participate in the General Assembly of a company limited by shares.

(2) The auditor shall have to examine all reports and statements, particularly the balance sheet and the inventory of properties which have been submitted to the supreme body of the business society, association, company and venture so as to check whether the said documents contain factual data, respectively whether they comply with the requirements of the statutory rules, and shall have to make a statement of his findings and opinion. No valid decision on the report can be taken unless his statement and or opinion has been made known.

para. 42

(1) Should the auditor have taken notice of the fact that some considerable decrease in the property/capital of the business society, association or venture can be expected or of a fact that may involve the liability as the present Law defines of the executive officers or the members of the Supervisory Board, he shall have to notify the Supervisory Board or in lack of such a Board, the business society, association, company or venture, and shall demand a meeting of the supreme body of the business society, association, company or venture.

(2) If the supreme body of the business society, association, company or venture has not been convoked, the auditor shall be entitled to convoke it. Should the supreme body of the business society, association, company or venture fail to take the necessary decisions, the auditor shall have to notify this fact to the Court of Registration.

Signing for the firm

para. 43

(1) Signing for the firm takes place so that the persons entitled to represent the business society, association, company or venture attach their own signature to the firm name of the business society, association, company or venture.

(2) The executive officers of the business society, association, company or venture are entitled to sign such a paper individually for the business society, association, company or venture – unless the Law has exceptionally otherwise provided – however, the signature of employees of the firm would be valid only if two employees invested with the title of representing the firm are jointly affixing their signatures.

(3) The persons entitled to represent the business society, association, company or venture shall have to submit their signatures after verification by a notary public to the Court of Registration or shall have to submit their signatures in person to the Court of Registration.

Revision of decisions on behalf of the business society, association, company or venture by the court

para. 44

(1) Any one of the members may demand the Court to revise a decision the business society, association, company or venture, or its bodies, have taken if the said decision infringes the provisions of the present Law or some other legislative rule, the articles of association (illegal decision). Also individuals defined concerning certain forms of business associations may demand this revision.

(2) The right of indent (1) shall not be entitled to the member who has approved by his vote the decision except in cases of error, fraud or threatening behaviour (Civil Code para. 210).

(3) The right referred to under indent (1) cannot be excluded in a valid manner and any waiving of this right should be considered as null and void.

para. 45

(1) An action against the unlawful (illegitimate) decision claiming its reconsideration shall be filed against the business society, association, company or venture within 30 days after taking the decision in question, under pain of forfeiture of the right. Initiation of the lawsuit has no delaying effect but the Court may suspend the execution of the decision.

(2) The Court revokes the decision infringing any law or the articles of association.

Liquidation of the company; squaring the account

Winding-up or liquidating the business society, association, company or venture

para. 46

(1) The company shall be considered wound up if
(a) the time of operation provided by the deed (articles) of association has expired or another condition of winding-up has ensued;
(b) the business society, association, company or venture decides its winding-up without nominating a successor;
(c) the business society, association, company or venture dissociates therefrom or transforms into another form of business society, association, company or venture;
(d) the number of the members has dropped to one (with the exception of the limited liability company and the company limited by shares) and no new member gets filed with the Court of Registration within 6 months;
(e) the Court of Registration has declared the state of Liquidation of the business society, association, company or venture;
(f) the Court dissolves the business society, association, company or venture by the winding-up procedure;
(g) Liquidation or winding-up is specified by the provisions of the present Law relating to certain forms of a business society, association, company or venture.

(2) The business society, association, company or venture shall cease to exist upon cancelling its entry in the Trade Register. Cancellation shall be published in the official gazette.

Squaring the account

para. 47

When a company is wound-up without a successor, squaring the account (liquidation) has to take place except if the winding-up proceedings are initiated because of permanent insolvency. The liquidation shall be carried out according to the statutory rules on the winding-up procedure – unless the present Law provides otherwise.

para. 48

(1) The liquidation is carried out by the executive officers of the business society, association, company or venture – except for the cases defined by indents (2) and (3) hereunder.

(2) Members representing at least one tenth of the votes may submit a petition to the Court of Registration to appoint another person for winding up the business society, association, company or venture.

(3) When winding-up of a business society, association, company or venture is declared (by the Court), the person in charge of winding-up is appointed by the Court of Registration.

(4) With the exception of cases defined by indents (2) – (3) initiation of the winding-up procedure and of the person in charge of winding-up the business society, association, company or venture – for the sake of entry and publishing.

para. 49

When appointing an individual in charge of winding-up the business society, association, company or venture, the Court of Registration
(a) may appoint such a natural person only who meets the requirements set by the present Law concerning an executive officer;
(b) may not appoint a natural person or legal entity against whom (which) the majority of the members of a business society, association, company or venture raises an objection.

para. 50

Upon designation (appointment) of a person in charge of winding-up, the right of the executive officers, representatives and employees of the business society, association, company or venture to sign for the firm ceases: their rights and duties are exercised by the person in charge of winding-up the business society, association, company or venture.

para. 51

(1) The person in charge of winding-up the business society, association, company or venture assesses the financial situation of the business society, association, company or venture, prepares the list of the creditors, compiles the company's final balance-sheet and submits all these to the supreme body of the business society, association, company or venture for approval.

(2) If, according to the judgement of the person charged with winding-up the business society, association, company or venture, the assets of the business society, association, company or venture do not even cover the claims of the known creditors, he shall be bound to initiate a winding-up procedure.

(3) In a winding-up procedure initiated because of the continuous and permanent insolvency of the business society, association, company or venture, the creditors thereof shall enjoy priority regarding the assets of the business society, association, company or venture against the creditors of the members.

para. 52

(1) The person in charge of winding-up the business society, association, company or venture shall.
(a) draw up a final balance-sheet and submit it to the supreme body of the business society, and then to the association, company or venture for approval.
(b) declare the termination of the procedure and notify the Court of Registration of his declaration and request the cancellation of the entry of the business society, association, company or venture in the Trade Register.

(2) The balance-sheet shall be accompanied by the report of the Supervisory Board or one auditor, if any.

para. 53

Any dispute arising between the person in charge of winding up the business society, association, company or venture and the members of the business society, association, company or venture shall be submitted for decision to the Court.

para. 54

Any claims raised against the business society, association, company or venture or its members, arising from the liabilities of the business society, association, company or venture, shall expire within five years from the winding-up of the business society, association, company or venture or of the membership, unless a statutory rule stipulates a shorter statutory limitation for a claim.

The various business societies, associations, companies and ventures

Chapter III. Unlimited partnership and deposit partnership companies

The unlimited partnership company

para. 55

(1) In a deed of association aimed at the formation of an unlimited partnership company the members of the company undertake the obligation to conduct business activities under their unlimited, joint and several liability and to make available the necessary assets for the company.

(2) The designation of 'unlimited partnership company' or its (Hungarian) abbreviation 'kkt' must be indicated in the name of the firm.

The foundation of an unlimited partnership company

para. 56

In the deed of association, in addition to the items listed in para. 21, indent (1) above, there shall be defined: the form of the members' (partners') contribution of assets, the value of the same, as well as the modes of their personal cooperation.

para. 57

(1) A body financed or supported by the State budget may not be party to an unlimited partnership company unless agreed to be such a member by its supervisory authority.

(2) A member of an unlimited partnership company may not be a member to any other business society, association, company or venture except to a company limit-

ed by shares – carrying on a similar business activity unless agreed to be such a member by the other partners.

(3) The provision of indent (2) above does not apply to a legal entity formed by an unlimited partnership company with persons employed by it (or members with duty to perform work).

para. 58

(1) If an activity is made conditional upon an official permit by a statutory rule, the unlimited partnership company may not pursue such an activity, except in case of possessing such a permit.

(2) The unlimited partnership company may pursue an activity subject to qualification only if among its members or employees there is at least one person who meets the requirements of qualification stipulated by statutory rules. A statutory rule may also require that all members of the unlimited partnership company pursuing an activity subject to qualification be in possession of the qualification so stipulated.

para. 59

(1) Members entitled to represent the unlimited partnership company are jointly required to notify the Court of Registration on the foundation of the company. Following such notification, the members may start the company's activities and may employ employees in this framework.

The internal legal relations of the unlimited partnership company

para. 60

(1) The member's contribution of assets supplied in cash or in consumables or in substitutable kind shall be transferred into the ownership of the unlimited partnership company. Other contributions of assets shall be transferred either into the ownership or the use of the unlimited partnership company, corresponding to the provisions of the deed of association. In case of doubt, the member's contribution of assets shall be deemed as the property of the unlimited partnership company.

(2) No interest on or remuneration (fee) after the contribution of assets may be stipulated with legal validity.

(3) In case of delay of paying a cash contribution, the member shall pay a 20 percent annual interest. In case of a delay in performing a non-financial contribution, the deed of association may even require payment of a penalty. Furthermore, the member or partner delaying his performance shall be liable for any damages arising to the unlimited partnership company by his delay.

(4) The property (assets) acquired by the unlimited partnership company in the course of its operation shall be the property of the unlimited partnership company.

para. 61

(1) None of the members can be requested to increase their contribution of

assets beyond the amount the deed of association stipulates, nor shall they be requested to complement the same if losses occur.

(2) During the validity of the membership relation, a member may not withdraw his contributed assets transferred for use by the unlimited partnership company, nor may he alienate or debit the same – unless with the joint consent of all members.

(3) Refunding the contribution of assets or their countervalue may only be claimed when winding-up the company or terminating the membership relation.

para. 62

(1) The company-members who are natural persons are bound to personally participate in the activities of the unlimited partnership company.

(2) Any stipulation exempting any such member from personal participation in the activities shall be null and void.

para. 63

(1) All members are entitled to partake in the management of the unlimited partnership company, except those who have been sentenced for a crime, with final effect to executable imprisonment, as long as not being absolved from the prejudicial legal consequences of being a previous offender.

(2) Any person whose sentence by a Court carries a prohibition from a profession, may not be entrusted with management of an unlimited partnership company pursuing the activity prohibited by the sentence, up to the term the sentence has stipulated.

para. 64

(1) In the deed of association the members may entrust one or several members with management; in such a case the other members are not entitled to management. Every member entitled to manage the company may act on his own in an independent manner.

(2) Each member entitled to management may protest against a measure planned by another member entrusted with management. In such a case the proposed measure – except for measures of pressing necessity – must be deferred until the members decide on it.

(3) If according to the deed of association, all or several of the members entitled to management must proceed jointly, then decisions shall be taken by a majority of votes. Pressing measures may be taken by anyone on his own, provided they are to protect the company from damage. The other members entitled to management must be informed of such a measure without delay.

(4) If a matter does not belong to the habitual business activity of the unlimited partnership company, decisions must be taken by all members even if the deed of association entrusts one or several members only with management.

para. 65

(1) A member entrusted with management may retire from this assignment according to the rules of normally giving notice (cf. para. 80).

(2) The other members of the unlimited partnership company may revoke the mandate (assignment) of management for an important reason. Important reasons are, in particular, a grave breach of duty in management, or unsuitability for discharging management duties.

para. 66

(1) The members shall take decisions in all matters affecting the unlimited partnership company by a majority of votes – with the exception of points (a) through (c) of indent (3). Every member shall have one vote.

(2) A unanimous vote is required in the following cases:

(a) Modification of the deed of association, with the exception of the cases defined by point (a) through (c) of indent (3);

(b) In matters beyond the scope of the habitual business activities of the unlimited partnership company;

(c) In other cases the deed of association provides.

(3) At least two-thirds majority of votes is required for the following decisions:

(a) Revocation of the mandate of management and entrusting another member with management;

(b) Revocation of the right of representation and appointment of a new representative;

(c) Exclusion of a member, including

(d) any other cases defined by the deed of association,

–   with the provision that in the cases defined by points (a) through (c) the member so affected may not vote.

(4) No valid stipulation deviating from the provisions of indent (2), points (a) through (b) and indent (3), points (a) through (c) may be made in the deed of association.

para. 67

(1) The member of the unlimited partnership company is entitled to supervise the management and to exercise the representation of the unlimited partnership company; In this context, he may personally request information on the state of affairs and shall have access to the books and other documents of the unlimited partnership company.

(2) The member entrusted with management or entitled to represent the unlimited partnership company shall regularly inform the other members on the affairs of the unlimited partnership company.

(3) Any deviation of the deed of association from the provisions of the above indents (1) and (2) shall be null and void.

para. 68

The unlimited partnership company may employ employees, home-workers, helping family members and vocational-school trainees (apprentices). The employer's
rights on behalf of the unlimited partnership company will be exercised by the
member appointed thereto by the members entitled to management.

para. 69

Each member shall be entitled to a remuneration for his personal cooperation
(work). Such remuneration must be shown among the liabilities of the unlimited
partnership company in the balance-sheet.

para. 70

(1) The unlimited partnership company shall draw up a balance-sheet and/or an
inventory of assets at the end of the year, out of which its financial status, the
changes of the latter, as well as the profit and loss can unequivocally be established.

(2) The members of the unlimited partnership company shall jointly share the
profits and bear the losses. Any stipulation excluding any member from the profit
or loss shall be null and void.

(3) Both profits and losses shall be divided among the members in proportion
with their respective contribution of assets.

External legal relations of the unlimited partnership company

para. 71

Each member shall be entitled to represent the unlimited partnership company,
except a member in respect of whom a cause of exclusion – as in para. 63 provides
– exists.

para. 72

(1) In the deed of association, the members may apoint one or several members
to represent the unlimited partnership company; in such a case the other members
will not be entitled to represent the company.

(2) If the unlimited partnership company has several representatives, each of
them may proceed on his own. The deed of association may also stipulate a joint
representation.

(3) Representatives of the unlimited partnership company shall exercise the right
of signing for the firm either alone or jointly – depending on whether they have the
right of sole or joint representation.

(4) The representative has full powers of representation. Any limitation of said
power would be ineffective in respect of any third person.

para. 73

(1) The appointed representative may waive this right according to the normal rules of giving notice (cf. para. 80).

(2) The other members of the company may, for an important reason, withdraw the right of representation from the designated representative. Important reasons are, in particular: a grave breach of duty by the representative, or his unsuitability for performing the duties of representation.

(3) The termination of the right of representation shall become effective in respect of third persons from the date of its entry into the Trade Register.

para. 74

(1) The liability of a member entitled to representation or management of the company shall be governed by the rules which apply to the liability of the executive officers of a business society, association, company or venture (cf. para. 32).

(2) The unlimited partnership company shall be liable for any damage which its representative may cause to third persons in the sphere of his capacity as a representative.

para. 75

(1) The unlimited partnership company shall primarily be responsible for any liabilities of the unlimited partnership company by the company's own property. Should the property of the unlimited partnership company fail to cover the liabilities, the members bear unlimited, joint and several liability by their own personal property. An exclusion or limitation of this liability in respect of third persons would be ineffective.

(2) A sentence may be passed against the company's assets, property even without proceeding against the individual members and the sentence can unconditionally be executed, but legal proceedings involving the personal properties (assets) of members would be practicable and executable solely if the members are subjects of the lawsuit. The members of the unlimited partnership company can be suited even jointly with the unlimited partnership company they are members to, without affecting their liabilities for the unlimited partnership company proper.

(3) A member entering an unlimited partnership company shall bear equal liability with the other members for the unlimited partnership company's debts (liabilities) of the unlimited partnership company arisen prior to his entry. Any stipulation deviating from this rule shall have no effect in respect of third persons.

para. 76

(1) Any creditor of a member may not retain or withhold as a security or as an indemnity any asset the member of the unlimited partnership company has trans-

ferred into the proprietorship of or for use by the unlimited partnership company. The creditor's claim may be covered only by that share which would be due to the member in case of winding-up the unlimited partnership company or terminating his membership. If the creditor has levied a distress upon the said part of assets, he may exercise the right of giving a normal notice (cf. para 80) due to the member, but may not claim surrendering the member's share to him in kind.

(2) A claim of the unlimited partnership company from any third person cannot be compensated for a claim of a member from the same third person, or inversely.

The termination of the membership relation and winding-up the unlimited partnership company

para. 77

The membership relation shall terminate by:
(a) common agreement (consensus) of members,
(b) exclusion,
(c) notice with immediate effect,
(d) normal notice,
(e) the member's death or winding up without any legal successor,
(f) when continuation of the membership contradicts or prevents the provision of a law.

para. 78

(1) A member can be excluded by the other members of the unlimited partnership company for an important reason. Important reasons are, in particular, if a member, in spite of being admonished in writing, fails to comply with his statutory or contractual obligations, or if his conduct to a great degree jeopardizes the fulfilment of the objectives of the unlimited partnership company, or if he is durably insolvent. The exclusion must be communicated with the member by indicating the reason.

(2) The affected member may not vote on the matter of exclusion.

(3) The member may file a complaint or an appeal with the court against the decision declaring his exclusion within 30 days of communicating with him such a decision. Failure to comply with this term involves the forfeiture of rights. Filing the action has no delaying effect on the exclusion.

para. 79

Any member may give notice of his membership with immediate effect if another member of the unlimited partnership company has committed a grave breach of the deed of association or has exercised a behaviour gravely endangering any further cooperation or jeopardizing the fulfilment of the objectives of the unlimited partnership company.

para. 80

(1) Any member may give a three months' notice of his membership in an unlimited partnership company founded for an indefinite period (normal notice). Any exclusion or limitation of this right would be null and void.

(2) If the term of the notice given falls at an unsuitable time, the other members may extend the term of notice by not more than a further three months.

para. 81

(1) When membership terminates upon consensus, exclusion, giving notice, or upon infringement of law, settlement with the member separating from the unlimited partnership company shall take place according to the status existing on the date of the termination of the membership; his due demand shall be refunded in money. His contribution transferred to the unlimited partnership company in any other form than finances shall be calculated at the value the deed of association stipulates or in lack of such a provision, at the market value prevailing at the time when he has made his contribution – unless returning his contribution in kind.

(2) If the member resigning from the unlimited partnership company as per indent (1) above has given his contribution for use by the unlimited partnership company, such a contribution shall be returned in kind, provided it still exists. The unlimited partnership company and the member in question may, however, agree otherwise.

(3) In lack of any contrary agreement, the share of assets due to the member resigning from the unlimited partnership company shall be refunded within three months from the termination of his membership.

para. 82

The inheritor of a deceased member or the legal successor of a member who has terminated his membership may join the unlimited partnership company as a member, subject to agreement with the other members. In lack of agreement, the provisions of para. 81 shall apply.

para. 83

(1) The member resigning from partnership company shall be liable – in an identical manner with the other members – for the debts of the unlimited partnership company towards third persons which have arisen up to the termination of his membership, for five subsequent years.

(2) The inheritor of a deceased member who does not join the unlimited partnership company will be liable for any debs of the unlimited partnership company which have arisen up to the date of death, according to the statutory rules on the liability for the testator's debts.

This provision shall apply according to the meaning and also to the legal successor of a member whose membership was terminated.

94

para. 84

If the unlimited partnership company has wound-up, the rules on the final account-ing (liquidation) shall apply, jointly with the complementary provisions of paras. 85 −86 hereunder.

para. 85

The tasks of final accounting (settlement) or liquidation shall be carried out by a person appointed by the members.

para. 86

(1) After settling the debts, before all, the value of the contributions by members shall be refunded − unless the deed of association provides otherwise. In the course of this, the non-financial contributions − unless refunding them in kind − shall be calculated at the value the deed of association provides or in lieu of any such provision, at the market value prevailing on contribution of the asset.

(2) The contribution invested in the company for use shall be returned in kind provided it still exists. By the wish of the member, the non-financial con-tribution which became the property of the company, may be returned in kind as well.

(3) After returning the contribution of the assets, the remaining property shall be divided among the members according to the contributions of assets.

Working teams

para. 87

(1) The working team is an unlimited partnership exclusively consisting of natu-ral persons.

(2) The name 'working team' − or its abreviation (in Hungarian: 'gmk') − must be indicated in the name of the firm.

(3) The rules relating to the unlimited partnership company shall apply to work-ing teams with the complementary provisions of paras. 88−89 hereunder.

(para. 87(3) taken out of force as of 1 April 1990)

para. 88

A working team may not carry on activities from which natural persons are barred by a Law, Law-decree or Decree of the Council of Ministers.

(para. 88 taken out of force as of 1 April 1990)

para. 89

In a working team the total number of the staff (members, employees and home-workers) may not exceed 500; Employees of the members shall equally be considered as members of the total number of the staff.

(para. 89 taken out of force as of 1 April 1990)

Working team operating under the responsibility of a legal entity

para. 90

(1) In respect of a working team exclusively consisting of employees and retired workers/employees of a legal entity and for the activities of which the said legal entity assumes liability (hereafter: working team operating under the liability of a legal entity) the rules relating to working teams shall apply with the amendment which paras, 91–93 hereunder define.

(2) The firm name of such a working team shall include the said legal entity whose liability has also to be entered in the Trade Register.

para. 91

(1) A working team operating under the liability of a legal entity may also be founded without any contribution of assets by its members.

(2) The foundation of a working team operating under the liability of a legal entity requires the preliminary assumption of liability on behalf of the legal entity. In the course of this act, the assumption of liability and the permission to use the assets of the legal entity may be subjected to certain conditions. However, a stipulation according to which the said working team may not conclude contracts with third persons, shall be invalid.

(3) The members of a working team operating under the liability of a legal entity shall bear liabilities for the obligations of the working team towards third persons only limited to the contribution of assets by the members, as well as by the total incomes the members have earned in the working team in the calendar year the given obligation arises. For any obligation of the working team that exceeds the foregoing the legal entity having assumed liability for the working team shall have to bear the responsibility: any limitation of the latter liability would be null and void.

para. 92

A working team operating under the liability of a legal entity may not employ any employee, worker, home-worker, helping family-member or vocational trainee (apprentice).

para. 93

(1) The legal entity may at any time, and without giving any reasons, withdraw its declaration of undertaking the liability for the working team, by a thirty days' notice. Such a withdrawal shall be reported to the Court of Registration, for entry and publication.

(2) Upon entering such a withdrawal, the working team operating under the liability of a legal entity terminates. Nevertheless the members may decide to contin-

ue the activities of the association according to the rules on working teams (paras. 87–89); This decision must be reported to the Court of Registration within thirty days of publishing the withdrawal of undertaking the liability on behalf of the legal entity, for entry and publishing by the Court of Registration. Failure to comply with this said term involves the forfeiture of rights.

The deposit partnership (Limited company)

para. 94

(1) The deposit partnership is founded by a need of association in which the members of the partnership undertake to pursue a joint business activity in such a manner that at least one of the members (full partner) will bear the unlimited liability jointly and severally with the other full partners, while the liability of at least one other member (external partner) will be limited to his contribution of asset(s) (deposit).

(2) The rules of an unlimited partnership company shall apply to the deposit partnership or limited company – unless the present Law provides otherwise.

(3) The denomination 'deposit partnership' or its abbreviation (in Hungarian: 'bt') must be shown in the name of the firm.

Foundation of the deposit partnership or limited company

para. 95

(1) If all full partners of the deposit partnership or limited company are natural persons, the rules relating to working teams shall apply according to the meaning.

(2) A State-budgetary body may become a full partner of a deposit partnership or limited company only with the consent of its supervisory authority.

(3) Instead of the contribution of assets by members of an unlimited partnership company, the term 'deposit of asset' shall apply to deposit partnership or limited company.

para. 96

The publication by the Court of Registration stating the registration of the deposit parnership or limited company may include – apart from the specified data – only the number of external partners and the amount of their assets deposited; the publication may not contain the names (firms) of external members unless agreed by them.

Internal relations within the deposit company (limited partnership company)

para. 97

(1) Solely full members shall compulsorily cooperate in person in activities

of the deposit company or limited partnership; the deed of association may,- however, entitle also external members with carrying on such activities. The renumeration or fee for the personal cooperation would be due also to the external partner.

(2) External members are not entitled for management of the company.

(3) The full and external members of the deposit company or limited partnership shall have to jointly decide on the following matters:

(a) Protesting against a planned measure of a member entitled to management of the company;

(b) On matters beyond the scope of the normal business activities of the company.

(4) Any contractual stipulations deviating from the contents of indents (2) and (3) shall be considered as null and void.

External legal relations of the company

para. 98

External members are not entitled to represent the company; any deviating contractual stipulation would be considered as null and void.

para. 99

The creditor of the company may initiate a lawsuit against the external member – except for the case which para. 100 (indent 1) governs – only in the case of the external member not providing contribution of assets the Trade Register indicates or if he has supplied with deposit only in part. The external member can be held responsible even in such a case only up to the value of his asset deposited according to the Trade Register.

para. 100

(1) If the firm name of the company indicates his name, even the external member is just as responsible as the full member.

(2) Upon an agreement with the other members of the company, the external member reduces the sum of his deposit, he shall be responsible up to the original sum against third persons until his new deposit has been entered in the Trade Register.

para. 101

The liability, i.e. responsibility of the external member joining the company for liabilities, debts of the company which have arisen before he joined the company shall be identical with those of the other external members. Any deviating arrangement with third persons would be considered as null and void.

98

Winding-up the company

para. 102

(1) The company shall be considered as terminated if any one of the full members separates from the company.

(2) If due to external members resigning from the company, only full members of the company will be left, but the deposit company may continue to proceed with its activities as an unlimited (mercantile) partnership (general partnership). Such a change in the company must be reported to the Court of Registration – for entry and publishing – within 30 days after the resignation of the last external member; any non-compliance with the said term would involve termination of the company.

Chapter IV. Association

para. 103

(1) An association is a business association which legal entities form for promoting the success of their business activities and for coordinating them as well as representing their branch interests. The association is not endeavouring to make its own profit and its members are responsible in an unlimited and several and joint manner for any debts or liabilities of the association that surpasses its assets.

(2) The association may carry out its services contributing towards the coordination tasks and any other joint business activity for fulfilling the joint, common objectives (which will be called herein–under: servicing and business activities).

(3) The designation 'association' shall be indicated in the firm name.

Foundation of the association

para. 104

(1) In addition to those listed in indent (1) of para. 21, the following items shall have to be determined in the deed of association:
(a) The objectives indenting to promote, respectively to coordinate the business management by members within the sphere of activity, as well as the objectives of representing the branch interests connected with the former activities;
(b) The distribution to members of bearing the operating costs and the method of accounting the costs;
(c) The conditions for refunding the asset due to the member when the member is resigning from the association;
(d) The system of distributing the residual assets following winding-up of the association;
(2) The deed of association shall provide on the following as necessary:
(a) The servicing and business activities:

(b) The extent of the assets of the association necessary for the servicing and business activities;

(c) The extent of the right of voting due to the various members within the frame of the servicing and business activities, the method of exercising this right and the method of procedure in the case of an equal number of votes;

(d) The rules of the participation of the profit of the serving and business activities;

(e) The supplies (secondary supplies) of other property value the various members have to bear, on the conditions of bearing the aforementioned as well as the extent of penalty payable upon failure of supplying or supplying to an insufficient degree the secondary supplies;

(f) Organization of the Supervisory Committee.

para. 105

The director shall be bound to report the foundation of the association for entry and publishing to the Court of Registration.

Rights and liabilities of members

para. 106

(1) The cost of operating the association shall be borne by the members and the members shall have to provide the assets (property) necessary for the servicing and business activities of the association as well.

(2) The members of the association may undertake the fulfilment of other services (secondary services) of property value as well. A separate remuneration (fee) shall be due to the member for secondary services (supplies); this remuneration or fee shall be shown in the balance of the association under the heading of the debts (liabilities) of the association.

para. 107

(1) The members are entitled to avail themselves of the services (supplies) provided by the association without any couterservices; they are due to participate in the profits of the servicing and business activities rendered to other parties.

(2) The profit arising in the course of the servicing and business activities shall be distributed in the proportion of the contribution of assets or property; otherwise profits shall be distributed at an equal proportion among the members.

Organization of the association
The board of directors

para. 108

(1) The controlling, governing organ of the association is the board of directors. Each member can appoint a representative to the board of directors.

(2) The scope of authority of the board of directors includes:

(a) Designing the order of controlling, guiding and supervising of the internal organization of the association;

(b) Determination of the strategy of the coordination and representation (of interests) as well as the servicing and business activities;

(c) Drawing up the balance of the association;

(d) Distribution of the profits arising from the servicing and business activities of the association;

(e) Making a decision which defines tasks the members have to carry out by their own management;

(f) Approving the contracts concluded on behalf of the association before entry into the Register;

(g) Deciding on winding-up, transforming, fusion, merger of the association or separation from another society, association, company or venture;

(h) Accepting the joining of the association;

(i) Election and recording the Director and exercising the rights of employers in connection with the Director;

(j) Should a Supervisory Committee operate in the association, election of the Supervisory Committee, recording or withdrawing the members of the said Committee and determining the fees of members;

(k) If an auditor is active in the association, appointment of the said auditor, withdrawal of his delegation and determining his fees;

(l) Amendment of the deed of association;

(m) Exclusion of a member;

(n) Decisions on all problems which according to the deed of contract belong to the sphere of authority of the Board of Directors.

para. 109

(1) The Board of Directors shall meet when necessary but at least once annually.

(2) The meetings of the Board of Directors shall be convoked by the Director. The representatives representing at least one tenth of the votes may at any time require the convoking the meeting of the Board of Directors, by stipulating the reason and the aim; should the Director fail to comply with this request within 30 days, the above said members may even convoke the meeting of the Board of Directors themselves.

para. 110

(1) The Board of Directors may decide solely on those questions which have been figuring in the invitation to the meeting. However, if all members are present at the meeting and they unanimously agree in discussing a problem not figuring in the invitation, an exception may be made of the former rule.

(2) The Board of Directors has a quorum if members representing at least three quarter parts of the total votes are present at the meeting. The deed of association may not depart from this stipulation in any legal manner.

101

para. 111

(1) In the sphere of coordination and interest representing activities, each member has one vote. As for the sphere of servicing and business activities as well as in the cases listed in the second sentence of indent (1) of para. 112, the extent of the right of voting shall be defined in proportion to the contribution of assets or in lieu of any such contribution of assets, the distribution should be of equal proportions.

(2) On making decisions, a member with whom the association shall have to conclude a contract by the decision or against whom a lawsuit shall have to be initiated as per the decision, may not vote.

para. 112

(1) The Board of Directors shall make its decisions by at least the simple majority of votes by the members present at the meeting. At least a three quarters majority of votes would, however, be necessary for deciding the winding-up, transformation, fusion or merger with another society, association, company or venture or separation from the said association, for accepting the joining of a new member and for excluding a member, and furthermore for amending the deed of association for any other reason.

(2) The deed of association may not legally depart from the stipulations of indent (1).

para. 113

(1) A majority of at least three quarters of votes is necessary for making a decision on behalf of the Board of Directors, which stipulates a liability of members to be carried out in the association's own business activity. The deed of association may not legally depart from this stipulation,

(2) The member is entitled to indemnity on behalf of the association for any damages which may arise from fulfilling his liability the Board of Directors has stipulated.

para. 114

(1) The Board of Directors may decide without even convoking a meeting.

(2) The draft of the decision proposed to be taken beyond the meeting shall have to be communicated with the members of the Board of Directors in written form, by defining a term of 15 days and the members of the Board shall submit their votes in written form. The Director shall inform the members of the results of voting within 8 days after the arrival of the last vote.

(3) The meeting for discussing the draft of the decision shall be convoked upon the request of any member of the Board of Directors.

para. 115

The members of the Board of Directors or their delegates may study the books and other documents of the association and may request information from the Director on the matters of the association.

para. 116

(1) The supervision by a court of any decision taken by the Board of Directors that infringes a Law may be requested, beyond the members of the Association, also by the Director and by any member of the Supervisory Board.

(2) If the Director initiates the suit, the association shall be represented by a member of the Supervisory Board, appointed by the Board itself. If no Supervisory Board operates in the association or if the lawsuit has been initiated by the Director and jointly by all members of the Supervisory Board, the court shall delegate a guardian ad litem to the association.

(3) The Provisions under Heading 4 of Chapter II shall apply, according to the meaning, otherwise to the supervision by a court of the decision infringing a Law.

The director

para. 117

(1) The director elected for a definite term shall have to manage the association – within the frame of the deed of association and the decisions taken by the Board of Directors – to his own, personal responsibility and shall represent the association towards third persons as well as before the Courts and other authorities. The Director may transfer his sphere of representation concerning a predefined group of subject-matters to some employees of the association as well.

(2) The employer's rights of the association shall be exercised by the Director. The Board of Directors may rule that the exercising of certain employer's rights related to leading executives of the association shall be subject to the agreement of the Board of Directors.

(3) The name and address of the Director, furthermore any changes in the person of the Director shall be reported to the Court of Registration for entry and publication.

The Supervisory Board

para. 118

(1) If justified by the number of members of the association, the significance or character of its activity justifies, the deed of association may organize a Supervisory Board consisting of at least 3 members. The members of the Supervisory Board shall be elected by the Board of Directors.

(2) The Supervisory Board shall convoke the meeting of the Board of Directors if the Director omits to do so or if the interest of the association otherwise requires its convocation.

Joining the association

para. 119

(1) Other legal entities may join the association according to the conditions of the deed of association.

(2) The Board of Directors shall decide on accepting the joining and shall simultaneously define the date of joining, the term of the involved liabilities as well as the extent of the right of the vote of the joining member within the sphere of the servicing and business activities of the association.

(3) The member joining the association shall be liable for any debts and liabilities which have arisen on behalf of the association before his joining it.

Resigning from (withdrawal from) the association

para. 120

(1) Any member may resign from the association by the end of the calendar year. The intent of resigning shall be announced to the Board of Directors at least 6 months before wishing to resign.

(2) The resigning member shall be liable for the debt arising before the date of his resigning from the association for at least 5 years from his withdrawal from the association.

para. 121

(1) The Board of Directors shall determine – within the frame of the deed of association – when and in what instalments it shall refund the asset the resigning member has contributed, together with the part of the asset the company has gained before the member's resigning to the member.

(2) Refunding shall be determined based on the balance of association in such a way that it should not jeopardize the further operation of the association, nevertheless, the term of refunding may not exceed one year.

(3) If refunding takes place at times other than when the member is resigning the association, a profit is due to the resigning member after the part of the asset which has not yet been refunded and in proportion with the said part of asset.

Exclusion

para. 122

(1) The Board of Directors can exclude (disbar) the member who has failed to comply with his liabilities the deed of association has defined in spite of a notice or summons in written form or if the member's further participation in the association would otherwise greatly infringe the interests of the association. The notice (summons) of exclusion shall be given by indicating the underlying reason.

(2) The affected member may not vote concerning the question of his exclusion.

(3) The member can appeal to a court against the decision stating his exclusion within 30 days from the date of obtaining notice from the said decision; Omission of this term entails the forfeiture of his right of appeal.

para. 123

(1) The rules concerning the resignation of the member shall govern the demands for assets of the excluded member and the pattern of refunding him.

(2) The excluded member shall be liable for any debts which have arisen before his exclusion from the association for five years from the date of his exclusion.

Winding-up the association

para. 124

The rules for final accounting upon winding-up the association without any successor shall be adopted together with the completions as per paras. 125 and 126.

para. 125

The Board of Directors decides on acquittal of the person in charge of final accounting (the Director) and the Supervisory Board simultaneously with approving the closing balance-sheet.

para. 126

After having settled the debts, the remaining assets shall have to be distributed in equal proportions among the members and if the members have contributed with assets to the association, distribution shall take place in proportion with the contributing assets.

Chapter V. The joint venture

para. 127

(1) The joint venture is a business society, association, company founded by legal entities the members of which are responsible for the liability of the said venture by the foundation capital and other assets of members they have made available for the joint venture. Should the assets of the enterprise fail to cover the debts, the members shall be jointly liable for the debts of the joint venture, in proportion to their contributed assets, as guarantors. The deed of association may legally and validly not define any more favourable liability or responsibility than the above said.

(2) The designation 'joint venture' – or the abbreviation thereof 'kv' (in Hungarian language) shall be indicated in the firm name of the venture.

Foundation of the company (venture)

para. 128

(1) In addition to the items listed in indent (1) of para. 21, the deed of association shall define the following:
(a) The organs (bodies) of the company (venture),
(b) the extent of the right of voting, the method of exercizing this right and the order of procedure when the number of votes is equal,
(c) the rules for sharing the profits and the rules for bearing losses,
(d) the conditions of refunding the asset due to the resigning member,
(e) the order of distribution of assets remaining upon winding-up the company (venture).
(2) The deed of association shall provide, as necessary, for the following:
(a) Defining the contributions other than financial to be provided by the various members and the values of such contributions,
(b) the services (secondary services) of other nature than assets the members have to bear, the conditions of such services and the extent of the penalty to be paid upon non-performance of the secondary service or upon unsatisfactory fulfilment of duties connected with the said secondary service,
(c) definition of a value of contract which if the countervalue of a contract to be concluded shall be solely within the scope of authority of the Board of Directors.

para. 129

In addition to supplying their contribution of assets, the members of the company/venture may undertake liabilities to provide other services (secondary services) of the value of an asset. The member shall be due to separate remuneration for secondary services; This should be indicated in the balance-sheet of the company/venture under the heading of the debts of the company/venture.

para. 130

The Director shall be bound to report the foundation of the company/venture to the Court of Registration for entry and publishing.

Rights and duties of members

para. 131

The members of the company/venture shall have to pay the financial contribution forming their share as well as to provide non-financial contribution and the secondary services they have undertaken.

para. 132

(1) Each member shall have a share in the profits of the company/venture and the member shall also jointly bear the losses. The member cannot be excluded from the profits nor from the losses. The deed of association may not legally deviate from these stipulations.

(2) The profits and losses shall be distributed among the members in proportion with their contributed assets.

Organization of the company/venture
The Board of Directors

para. 133

(1) The controlling body or organ of the company/venture shall be the Board of Directors. Each member shall delegate a representative to the Board of Directors.

(2) The scope of authority of the Board of Directors include the following:

(a) Designing the control and supervisory order of the internal organization of the company/venture;

(b) Approval of the plans and financial strategy of the company/venture;

(c) Statement of the company/venture balance-sheet and distribution of profits;

(d) Deciding on winding-up the company/venture, its transformation, fusion or merger with other societies, associations, companies, ventures and or separation therefrom;

(e) Accepting the joining of new members;

(f) Election and revoking (withdrawal) of the director and exercising the employer's rights connected with the director;

(g) Electing the Board of Directors, revoking the members of the Board of Directors and approving the rules of procedure (management) of the Board of Directors, provided a Board of Directors operates within the frame of the company/venture;

(h) If a Supervisory Board is operating within the frame of the company/venture, electing the Supervisory Board, revoking the members of the Supervisory Board – except for the case regulated by indent (3) of para. 143 –, furthermore approving the rules of procedure (management) and the remuneration (fee) of members;

(i) If an auditor is operating within the frame of the company, appointing the auditor, revoking the auditor's commission and determination of his remunerations/fees;

(j) Decisions on concluding or amending such contracts the value of which surpasses the extent the deed of association provides and of contracts the company/venture concludes with its own members; The latter mentioned provision is not applicable if conclusion of such contracts belong to the usual activities of the company/venture;

(k) Approval of contracts concluded on behalf of the company/venture before entry of the company in the Trade Register;

(l) Amendment of the deed of association;

(m) Exclusion of a member;
(n) Decision on all matters the deed of association has allocated to the sphere of authority of the Board of Directors.

para. 134

(1) The Board of Directors shall hold meetings as necessary but at least once a year.

(2) The meetings of the Board of Directors shall be convoked by the Director, by communicating the agenda with the members of the Board. Members of the Board representing at least one tenth part of the votes may require convoking the meeting of the Board of Directors at any time, by indicating the cause and the objective; Should the Director fail to comply with this demand within 30 days, the members of the Board may even convoke themselves the meeting of the Board of Directors.

para. 135

(1) The Board of Directors may decide solely on questions which are figuring in the invitation the Board has sent to its members for the meeting; Except for the case where all members of the Board are present at the meeting and unanimously agree in negotiating a question of the agenda not figuring in the invitation.

(2) The Board of Directors has a quorum when Board members representing at least three quarter parts of the votes are present at the meeting. The deed of association may not legally deviate from this provision.

(3) The members are entitled to vote in proportion with their contribution of assets.

(4) The member with whom a contract shall be concluded according to the decision or the member who must be suited may not vote when making the decision.

para. 136

(1) The Board of Directors decides by at least the simple majority of votes of members present at the meeting. At least a three quarters majority of votes is necessary for deciding on winding-up the company/venture, its transforming, merger or fusion with some other society, association, company, venture and or separation from the afore said, for approving the joining of a new member and for excluding a member, furthermore for amending the deed of association for any other reason.

(2) The deed of association may legally not deviate from the provisions of indent (1).

para. 137

(1) The Board of Directors may even come to decisions without holding a meeting.

(2) The draft decision proposed beyond the meeting shall be submitted to the members of the Board of Directors in written form, by setting out a term of 15 days

and the members of the Board shall submit their votes in written form. The director shall inform the Board members within 8 days following the receipt of the last vote on the results of the vote.

(3) The meeting shall be convoked to discuss the draft decision upon the request of any of the members of the Board of Directors.

para. 138

The members of the Board of Directors or their authorized representatives may inspect the books and other documents of the company/venture and may ask the director to supply them with information on matters of the company/venture.

para. 139

(1) In addition to members of the company/venture, any member of the Board of Directors or of the Supervisory Board can file a suit with the Court for supervising an illegal decision which infringes a law made by the Board of Directors.

(2) If the Director files the lawsuit, the company/venture shall be represented at the Court by a member of the Supervisory Board appointed by the Board. If no Supervisory Board is acting in the company/venture or if the Director and all members of the Supervisory Board jointly file the lawsuit, the Court shall designate a fiduciary or trustee (administrator) to the company/venture.

(3) The provisions under Heading 4 of Chapter II shall apply, according to the meaning, otherwise to the supervision by the Court of the decision infringing a law.

Board of Management

para. 140

(1) The deed of association may provide for establishing a Board of Management if the number of members of the company/venture justifies such a measure. The members to the Board of Management shall be elected by the Board of Directors from among its members for a predetermined period of time and may revoke these members at any time.

(2) The sphere of activity of the Board of Management shall be definied in the deed of association. The sphere of activity determined under points (d), (g), (h), (i), (l), and (m) of indent (2) of para. 133 may, however, not be delegated, or transferred to the Board of Management. The deed of association may not legally deviate from the latter mentioned provision.

para. 141

(1) The Board of Management shall proceed in an independent manner within the frames of the deed of association, and the decisions of the Board of Directors it shall determine its order of procedures itself, and the latter shall be approved by the Board of Directors.

(2) The Board of Management shall annually submit a report on its activities to the Board of Directors. The Board of Directors may at any time request the Board of Management to give an account or report.

(3) The director or any member of the Supervisory Board may submit a petition to the Board of Directors against any illegal decision (infringing the law) the Board of Management has taken.

The Director

para. 142

(1) The company/venture shall be controlled by the director subject to his own, individual responsibility and shall represent the company/venture against any third persons as well as at Courts and other authorities; The director shall conduct his above-mentioned activities within the frame of the deed of association and the decisions of the Board of Directors and the Board of Management. The director can transfer his right of representation to employees of the company/venture, concerning a certain defined group of matters.

(2) The director shall exercise the employer's rights of the company. The exercise of certain employers' rights concerning executives in leading positions of the company can be retained by the Board of Directors or can be made subject to approval of the Board of Management.

(3) The name and address of the directors, furthermore any changes taking place in the person of the director shall be reported to the Court of Registration for entry in the Trade Register and for publishing.

The Supervisory Board

para. 143

(1) If the number of members, the significance of activity or character of the company justifies, the deed of association may provide for a Supervisory Board consisting of not less than 3 members.

(2) In the case regulated by indent (1), the members of the Supervisory Board shall be elected by the Board of Directors; The Board of Directors may not elect any employee/worker of the company as a member of the Board.

(3) Organization of a Supervisory Board shall be mandatory if the number of full-time employees/workers of the company/venture surpasses 200 hands on the annual average.

para. 144

(1) The Supervisory Board may convoke a meeting of the Board of Directors, respectively the Board of Management if the Director fails to convoke such a meeting or if the interest of the company/venture otherwise requires convoking the meeting.

(2) If the opinion of representatives of employees/workers differs from that of

the Board in the Supervisory Board, this minority opinion should also be expounded on in the course of the meeting of the Board of Directors (Board of Management).

Joining the Company/Venture

para. 145

(1) Corresponding to the conditions of the deed of association, other legal entities may similarly enter the company/venture (joining).

(2) The Board of Directors (Board of Management) shall decide on initiating the joining and the said Board shall simultaneously define the date of joining, the term of fulfilling the involved liabilities and the extent of the right of vote of the member joining the company/venture.

para. 146

(1) The member joining the company/venture shall be responsible for any of the company/venture-debts which have arisen before his joining, The member joining the company may limit his liability on joining the company by a statement addressed to the Board of Directors (Board of Management); In which case, he shall be responsible for debts which have arisen before his joining the company only by his/its own contributed assets.

(2) Limitation of the liability as per indent (1) shall be entered in the Register; This limitation shall be effective with respect to third persons from the day of entering it in the Register.

Resignation

para. 147

(1) The member may resign from the company/venture at the end of the year. The intent of resigning shall be reported to the Board of Directors (Board of Management) at least 6 months prior to doing so.

(2) The resigning member shall be responsible for any debts which have arisen before his resigning for five years from the date of resigning.

para. 148

(1) The Board of Directors (Board of Management) shall determine, within the frames of the deed of association, when and by what instalments it intends to refund the contribution of assets and the proportion the resigning member has achieved of the assets before resigning the company/venture to the resigning member.

(2) Any refunding shall be determined based on the balance-sheet of the company/venture so that it may not jeopardize any further operation of the company/venture but the term of refunding may not exceed 3 years.

(3) If refunding does not take place upon resignation, profits are due to the resigned member in proportion with the yet unrefunded portion of assets.

para. 149

A member may resign from the company/venture also by transferring the rights of association to another member. In such a case, the resigned member shall not be responsible to the company/venture for any debts which arose before his resignation.

Exclusion

para. 150

(1) The Board of Directors may exclude a member who/which has failed to comply with his liability the deed of association has defined, not even upon written summons, or if his further participation in the joint company/venture would otherwise gravely infringe the interest of the joint company/venture. The excluded member shall be notified of his exclusion by also indicating the underlying reason of exclusion.

(2) The affected member may not vote on the question of exclusion.

(3) Within 30 days after communicating the decision of exlusion to him, the member may file a petition against the decision stating his exclusion to the Court; Omission of this term would entail the loss of the right. The filing of a lawsuit has no delaying effect on the exclusion.

para. 151

(1) The rules concerning resignation shall govern the demands for assets of the excluded member and to the order of refunding.

(2) The excluded member shall be responsible for 5 years from his exclusion for any company/debts which arose before his exclusion.

Termination (winding-up) of the company/venture

para. 152

If the company/venture is terminated (wound-up) without any legal successor, the rules and regulations concerning final accounting shall apply with the completions of paras. 153-154.

para. 153

The Board of Directors shall decide, simultaneously with approving the closing balance-sheet, on discharging, releasing the person in charge of the final accounting (the Director) and the Supervisory Board.

para. 154

The assets remaining after settling the debts shall be distributed among the members in proportion with their contributed assets.

Chapter VI. The limited liability company

para. 155

(1) The limited liability company is a business company where the founding primary capital consists of primary deposits of predetermined values wherein the liability of members towards the company covers the supply of the primary deposit to the company and other contribution of assets to the company which the deed of association may possibly define. The member is not responsible for any liabilities of the company.

(2) The designation limited liability company or its abbreviation 'kft' (in Hungarian language) shall be shown in the firm name of the company.

Foundation of the company

para. 156

(1) Even a single member may found the company (one-man company).

(2) The canvassing of members or partners by public advertising or invitation is prohibited.

para. 157

(1) In addition to those listed in indent (1) of para. 21, also the following items should be determined in the deed of association:
(a) the size (magnitude) of the basic capital and the basic deposits of the various members/partners;
(b) the method and term of paying deposits in term of money which have not yet been fully settled;
(c) the extent of the right to voting and the procedure to be followed in the case of equality of votes;
(d) the first manager, respectively in case of several managers, the method of management and representation, furthermore the method of signing for the firm;
(e) the members of the first supervisory board when organization of a supervisory board is mandatory;
(f) the person of the first auditor if election of an auditor is mandatory.

(2) The deed of association shall determine, if necessary, the following:
(a) the non-financial deposits and their respective values;
(b) any other services (secondary services) having no value of an asset which the members have to provide, their respective conditions and the extent of the penalty to be paid in case of non-fulfilment or improper fulfilment of the secondary services;

(c) authorization of the meeting of members to specify additional payment;

(d) in case of succession of title, the exclusion of the transfer of the share in business and the distribution of the share of business;

(e) the permission of withdrawing a share in business;

(f) authorization of all members/partners concerning management and representation;

(g) limitation of the right of representation of managers;

(h) establishing a Supervisory Board if the organization of such a Board is not mandatory;

(i) election of the auditor if electing an auditor is not mandatory.

(3) A foundation deed should be issued for foundation of a one-man limited-liability company. The rules and regulations concerning the deed of association shall apply, according to the meaning, and to the contents of the foundation deed. Where the present Law provides concerning the deed of association, it should be considered for providing also for the deed of foundation.

para. 158

(1) The basic capital of the limited-liability company consists of the totality of the basic deposits of the various members.

(2) The sum of the basic capital may not be less than Ft 1,000.000.

para. 159

(1) The basic deposits of members/partners may amount to various sums but the amount of any basic deposit may not be less than Ft 100.000. The basic deposit should be deposit defined in forint and its sum should be divisible by ten thousand, without any remainder.

(2) Each member/partner shall have one basic deposit; one basic deposit may, however, have even several owners.

para. 160

Th sum of deposited moneys on foundation of the limited liability company may not be less than 30 % of the basic capital, respectively Ft 500.000.

para. 161

(1) The foundation of the limited liability company should be reported to the Court of Registration for entry and publication. The report shall have to be submitted jointly by all managers. In case of a one-man limited liability company, it shall be reported that the company has but a single founder.

(2) The report to the Court of Registration may take place only after at least one half of each deposit in terms of money has been paid, respectively in the case of a one-man company, when the full amount of the deposit has been paid, respectively if the deposit of non-financial character has been made available in full to the company.

(3) If the total sum of money deposits have not been paid upon foundation of the company, the term and method of paying the residual sums shall be determined in the deed of foundation. Within one year after having registered the limited liability company in the Register, all deposits in terms of money must be paid; the deed of association may not legally deviate from this provision.

para. 162

(1) If an auditor operates in the limited liability company, it shall be prohibited to determine the value of the deposit of non-financial character at a value higher than the auditor defines.

(2) Those members of the limited liability company which have made the company to accept a deposit in kind of a member at a value surpassing the real value in spite of the fact that they have known this circumstance, or who have proceeded on the course of founding the limited liability company in any other fraudulent manner shall be responsible for any resultant damage without any limitation and jointly. Any exemption from this responsibility shall be null and void from the aspect of creditors of the limited liability company.

Legal relations between the company and the members/partners

para. 163

(1) The members/partners of the limited liability company shall be bound to pay the deposits in terms of money and to put at the company's disposal the deposits in kind.

(2) The members of the limited liability company may not be exempted from the compulsory payment of deposits and any comprisal (compensation) on behalf of the limited liability company is impermissible. The deed of association may legally not deviate from this provision.

para. 164

(1) The member/partner who has failed to pay the sum due to cover the basic deposit at the term which the deed of association has defined, shall be required to pay an annual interest of 20 per cent to the limited liability company.

(2) In case of a delay, the member/partner shall be summoned to fulfil his obligation by setting out an additional term of not less than 30 days. The summons should indicate that failure to comply with the new term would involve the loss of his former payments made to cover his basic deposit and the exclusion from the limited liability company.

(3) In case of failure of the additional term, the limited liability company excludes the member/partner. The company shall have to notify the member/partner of his exclusion.

(4) The partner/member whose membership/partnership in the limited liability company has terminated according to indent (3) shall be liable for any damage, which his omission of payment has resulted, to the limited liability company.

para. 165

(1) The limited liability company shall sell the business share (para. 169) of the excluded member by way of public aution. Selling the business share by any other way should be agreed by the excluded member/partner.

(2) From the settled sales receipt, before all the overdue claim of the limited liability company covering the unpaid part of the basic deposit of the excluded member/partner while the residual amount is due to the excluded member/partner.

para. 166

(1) If selling the business share proves to be impossible by the method para. 165 provides, the limited liability company may redeem, i.e. cancel the said business share, or the other members/partners of the limited liability company shall have to pay the full amount of the basic deposit of the excluded member to the company, in proportion with their own basic deposits. The basic deposit of each member shall increase in proportion with the sums so paid.

(2) Upon redeeming, i.e. cancelling the business share, respectively payment of the basic share on behalf of the other members/partners, the excluded member may claim only the proportion of that proportion of his business share which he has paid for.

para. 167

(1) In excess of supplying their basic deposits, the members/partners of the limited liability company may undertake liabilities concerning execution of other services (secondary services) in kind. Any personal cooperation by members/partners which they carry out in their capacities, other than officers or office-bearers of the limited liability company, shall qualify as a secondary service.

(2) A separate remuneration (fee) is due to the partner/member for secondary services; any such remuneration/fee should be indicated in the balance-sheet of the company as a debt of the company.

para. 168

(1) The deed of association can authorize the general meeting of members/partners to specify additional compulsory payments for the members/partners so as to cover losses. The deed of association shall define the highest sum the payment of which can compulsorily be claimed from the member/partner. Any additional payment shall not increase the basic deposit of the member/partner.

(2) Additional payments shall be defined and made in proportion with the basic deposits. An additional payment can be called for even before the full payment of the basic deposit.

(3) The provisions of paras. 164 and 165 shall apply according to the meaning in case of delayed additional payment, however, with the difference that the sum of

the additional payment not made, and which is due to the limited liability company, shall be subtracted from the sales price of the business share.

para. 169

(1) Subsequent to registry of the limited liability company, the rights of members/partners and the shares due to them from the assets of the limited liability company will be embodied by the business share. The extent of the business share shall be adapted to the basic deposits by members/partners.

(2) Each member may have only a single business share. If the member/partner acquires additional business shares, his business share increases in proportion with the acquired business shares.

(3) One business share may even have several owners. These owners shall be considered as one member/partner within the limited liability company; They may exercise their rights only by their joint representative and they shall jointly be responsible for the liabilities of a member.

para. 170

The business share can freely be transferred to members of the limited liability company. Any agreement on behalf of the limited liability company is necessary only if the business share compulsorily requires also secondary services.

para. 171

(1) The business share may be transferred to an outsider only if the member has fully settled his basic deposit. A member/partner, the limited liability company or a person appointed by the general meeting of members (in this order) shall have the right of preemption (privilege of purchasing before others) for the business share intended to be transferred.

(2) The limited liability company can purchase for its own purposes the business share from its own assets over and above the basic capital.

(3) Should a member, the limited liability company or the appointed person fail to declare himself/itself within 15 days taken from the day of reporting the intent of transferring the business share, it should be considered that he/it has agreed to the transfer. This provision shall apply also to the case which the second sentence of para. 170 regulates.

para. 172

The deed of association may not define any more favourable rules for transferring the business share than paras. 170 and 171 provide.

para. 173

When alienating the business share of a member/partner in the course of a procedure conducted by the court-bailiff, the other members/partners, the limited liability company, respectively a person the general meeting of members/partners has appointed shall have a preemption right for the business share, in the said order of persons/entities.

para. 174

(1) When transferring a business share, the rights and liabilities from the membership/partnership relation of the person transferring the business share shall be vested in the person/entity acquiring the said business share.

(2) The transfer of a business share does not call for amending the deed of association.

(3) The change in ownership and its date shall be reported by the purchaser to the limited liability company, for entry in the list of members/partners (para. 201). The report shall be made by the purchaser either in the form of an official (authentic) act or a private deed and the purchaser/buyer shall state in the said document or deed that he considered the provisions of the deed of association as mandatory for himself.

para. 175

Upon decease or winding-up of the member/partner, his business share devolves upon his successor. Should the deed of association exclude the devolution, the deed shall provide for purchasing the business share on behalf of the members/ partners. In lack of such a provision, the business share shall have to be cancelled – by refunding its value – by applying the rules concerning reducing the basic capital.

para. 176

(1) The business share can be distributed solely in the case of a transfer, the legal succession of terminated membership/partnership or inheritance. The division calls for the agreement of the limited liability company.

(2) The rules concerning the least extent of the basic deposit shall apply even in the case of dividing business shares.

(3) The deed of association may exclude the possibility of dividing a business share.

para. 177

(1) During the life of the limited liability company, the members/partners may not require the limited liability company to refund the basic deposits; Their rights are limited to the divisible part of the profits as per balance-sheet of the limited liability company. The deed of association may legally not deviate from this provision.

(2) The profits shall be distributed among the members/partners in proportion with the business shares.

para. 178

(1) From the assets necessary for covering the basic capital, the limited liability company may not execute any payments in favour of members/partners – except for the remunerations (fees) for secondary services and the reduction of the basic capital. The deed of association may legally not deviate from this provision.

(2) Any additional payments not needed for making up for losses shall have to be paid back to the members/partners. Any refunding may take place solely if the members/partners have fully settled the values of their basic deposits. The deed of association may legally not deviate from the last mentioned provision.

(3) Any payments made in spite of the provisions of indents (1) and (2) shall have to be refunded to the limited liability company. The managers, members of the Supervisory Board and auditors who have failed to proceed with the care generally expected from persons filling these respective positions, concerning the making of the payment, shall be jointly responsible for the repayment, together with the member who obtained any such refund.

para. 179

(1) The limited liability company may purchase up to one third part of the business shares from its assets over and above the basic capital, provided the general meeting of members/partners has decided so, by at least a majority of three quarter parts. Only such business shares may be purchased, upon which the full amount of basic deposits have been paid.

(2) The business share purchased according to indent (1), the limited liability company shall have to sell within one year from the date of purchase or shall have to cancel any such share by applying the rules concerning the reduction of the basic capital.

(3) The business share that has come into the ownership of the limited liability company does not involve any right of voting and it should also be left unconsidered when calculating the quorum; Any profits due to such business shares shall have to be distributed among the members/partners when the limited liability company is winding up.

(4) The deed of association may legally not deviate from the provisions of indents (1) through (3).

para. 180

(1) Withdrawal, cancellation of the business share is justified upon exclusion of a member/partner, upon the limited liability company acquiring the business share and furthermore whenever the deed of association permits such withdrawal or cancellation. In the latter mentioned case, the business share may be withdrawn/cancelled without any agreement by the member/partner affected by such withdrawal or cancellation if the deed of association has contained the conditions of cancelling/withdrawing the business share at the time when the member/partner has acquired the said business share.

(2) Should cancellation/withdrawal of the business share result in reducing the basic capital, then cancellation/withdrawal may be affected solely by reducing the basic capital.

para. 181

The one-man limited liability company may not purchase any of its business shares for its own purposes and may not withdraw/cancel any business shares.

para. 182

(1) The general meeting of members/partners may decide, by at least a three quarters majority of votes, to exclude a member/partner who has failed to comply with his liabilities the deed of association defines in spite of a written summons or a member/partner whose retention within the limited liability company may greatly endanger attainment of the objectives of the company. The exclusion shall be communicated with the partner/member by indicating also its reason; The deed of association may legally not deviate from this provision.

(2) To affected member/partner may not vote on the question of his exclusion.

(3) The member/partner may file a complaint with the Court against the decision stating his exclusion within 30 days after having communicating with him the said decision; Omission of this term would involve forfeiture of the said right. The initiation of the suit shall have no delaying effect on the exclusion.

(4) The provisions of para. 165 shall apply, according to the meaning, to the sale of the business share of the excluded member/partner. The limited liability company may cancel/withdrawal the business share if the said business share cannot be sold in the way as para. 165 provides.

Organization of the limited liability company
General meeting of members/partners

para. 183

(1) The general meeting of members/partners is the supreme organ of the limited liability company which shall have the right to decide also on questions belonging to the sphere of authority of its other organs. The general meeting of members/ partners shall be convoked at least once a year.

(2) The exclusive sphere of authority of the general meeting of members/partners includes the following:

(a) Definition of the balance-sheet and distribution of results/profits;
(b) Passing a decree on additional payment and refunding any such payment;
(c) Division and cancellation/withdrawal of business shares;
(d) Exclusion of a member/partner;
(e) Electing the managers, withdrawal of the (discharging) managers and determining the remuneration (fee) of managers, and the exercise of the employer's rights concerning managers;
(f) Election and withdrawal of the members of the Supervisory Board and deter-

mining their remunerations (fees) except for the case in which indent (2) of para. 209 regulates;

(g) Approving the conclusion of a contract the value of which surpasses at least one quarter part of the basic capital, respectively of a contract which the limited liability company concludes with its own members/partners, managers or any near relative thereof (point b) of para. 685 of the Civil Code except in the case of the conclusion of the last mentioned contract belonging to the usual activity of the limited liability company;

(h) Approval of contracts concluded on behalf of the limited liability company before its entry in the Register;

(i) Enforcement of claims for damages against members/partners responsible for the foundation of the limited liability company, against managers and members of the Supervisory Board, furthermore, taking measures on the representation of the limited liability company in lawsuits initiated against managers;

(j) Decisions on winding up, transformation, fusion, merger and separation of the limited liability company;

(k) Amendment of the deed of association;

(l) All matters which the present Law or the deed of association provides to be within the exclusive sphere of authority of the general meeting of members/partners.

(3) The deed of association may legally not deviate from the provisions of points (a) through (k) of indent (2).

para. 184

The general meeting of members/partners shall not be operative in the case of a one-man limited liability company, the founder shall have to exercise the sphere of authority of the said meeting.

para. 185

Another duly authorized member/partner may similarly represent the member/partner in the general meeting of members/partners. The manager and a member of the Supervisory Board may not act as a representative. The representation should be comprised either in an official/notarial document (deed) or a private document of probative force.

para. 186

(1) Unless the present Law or the deed of association provides otherwise, the general meeting of members/partners decides by the simple majority of votes of members/partners present at the said meeting. Every Ft 10 000 of the paid-up business shares entitles the member to one vote.

(2) The general meeting of members/partners forms a quorum if at least one half of the basic capital is represented at the event. The deed of association may not legally deviate from this provision.

(3) If the general meeting of members/partners could not form the quorum, the

said meeting again convoked for the above reason shall have a quorum concerning matters on the original agenda irrespective of the extent of the basic capital which the members/partners present represent.

para. 187

(1) The extent of the right of voting and the procedure for the case of an equal number of votes shall have to be regulated in the deed of association. Ten votes are, however, due to each member and the deed of association may legally not deviate from this provision.

(2) The member/partner whom the decision has exempted from liabilities or responsibilities or who has been given by such a decision some other favour to the detriment of the company, furthermore with whom a contract has to be concluded according to the decision, respectively against whom a lawsuit has to be initiated or who is otherwise interested or affected may not vote. The deed of association may legally not deviate from the above provisions.

para. 188

The members who have brought a decision of which they have been aware or of which they could know considering the care that could be expected from them that the said decision evidently infringes significant interests of the limited liability company, shall be responsible without any limitation and jointly for any resultant damage.

para. 189

(1) Unless the present Law or the deed of association provide otherwise, the managers shall have to convoke the general meeting of members/partners. This right shall be due to the managers even if the present Law or deed of association provides that some other person or entity shall also be entitled to convoke the general meeting of members/partners.

(2) In addition to the cases which the present Law or the deed of association provide, the general meeting of members/partners shall be convoked also in the case where that is otherwise necessary for the interests of the company. The general meeting of members/partners shall be convoked immediately, without any delay, if the balance-sheet of the limited liability company reveals that the basic capital has dropped to one half of its initial value due to some loss.

(3) In the case of a one-man limited liability company, the founder shall be requested for his decision instead of convoking the general meeting of partners/members.

para. 190

(1) Members/partners representing at least one tenth part of the basic capital can request in written form - by indicating the reason and the objective - convocation of the general meeting of members/partners. Should the manager fail to comply with

this request within 8 days or if there is no person whom the request can be addressed, the members/partners can themselves convoke the general meeting of members/partners.

(2) The general meeting of partners/members shall have to decide whether the cost due to organizing the general meeting of members/partners convoked according to indent (1) shall have to be borne by the limited liability company.

para. 191

(1) The members/partners shall be invited to the general meeting of members/partners by communicating with them the agenda. A period of not less than 15 days should elapse from mailing (sending) the invitations and the day of the general meeting of members/partners.

(2) Unless the general meeting of members/partners has regularly been convoked, the meeting can pass a decision only if all members/partners are present and if no protest has been launched against the general meeting of partners/members take place.

(3) Any one of the members (partners) is entitled to request the negotiation of a question on the agenda he desires. He shall have to expound on his proposal at least 3 days before the general meeting of members/partners. Questions not figuring in the invitation to the meeting, respectively which have not been stated to the members/partners can be discussed by the general meeting of members/partners only if all members/partners are present and none of them protest against discussing it.

(4) The deed of association may not legally deviate from the provisions of indents (1) through (3)

para. 192

(1) The members/partners can make decisions even without holding a general meeting of members/partners.

(2) The draft of any proposal a partner/member wishes to submit beyond the general meeting of members/partners should be communicated with the members/partners in writing, by setting out a term of 15 days; The members/partners shall submit their votes in writing. The managers shall have to inform the members/partners on the result of voting and on the decision as well as on the date of the said decision within 8 days after the arrival of the last vote.

(3) The general meeting of members/partners should be convoked for discussing the draft decision if any of the members so desire.

para. 193

(1) The manager and any member of the Board of Supervisors may demand the supervision of any illegal decision that infringes a law the general meeting of members/partners has passed.

(2) The suit should be submitted to the Court by the manager and the limited liability company should be represented at the Court (in the lawsuit) by a member of the Supervisory Board whom the said Board has appointed. If the limited liability

company has no Supervisory Board, the lawsuit shall have to be submitted by all managers and all members of the Supervisory Board jointly and the Court shall delegate a trustee (administrator) to the limited liability company.

(3) The provisions under Heading 4 of Chapter II shall apply, according to the meaning, otherwise to the supervision by the Court of a decision infringing the Law.

para. 194

(1) The managers shall keep a continuous register of the decisions the general meeting of members/partners are passing (log of decisions). Once a decision has been taken, it should be entered into the log of decisions by the managers. The decision is valid solely after this entry and one of the members/partners who has participated in passing the decision shall certify it by his signature.

(2) Any member/partner may inspect the log of decisions and may request a certified copy of the decisions (the copy has to be certified by the managers).

(3) In the case of a one-man limited liability company, the decisions of the founder should be recorded in the log of decisions only f the founder is not in charge of managing the company.

para. 195

(1) If the general meeting of members/partners has rejected the proposal according to which an expert (auditor) shall examine the balance-sheet of the last year of any other event which has occurred in the management of the two past years, respectively if the general meeting of members/partners has omitted to make a decision on the question of a regularly submitted proposal on the said matter, the Court of Registration can rule, at the demand of members/partners representing at least one tenth part of the basic capital, the execution of such a supervision.

(2) The demand shall have to be submitted within 30 days after the date of the general meeting of members/partners. Omission of this term would involve the loss of all rights.

para. 196

(1) If the general meeting of members/partners has rejected the proposal according to which a claim for indemnification should be lodged against the members/partners responsible for foundation of the limited liability company, against managers or members of the Supervisory Board and auditors furthermore, that a claim for indemnification against the majority of members should be enforced by application of para. 188, respectively if the general meeting of members/partners has omitted to pass a decision on such a proposal which has regularly been submitted, members representing at least one tenth part of the base capital may require the Court to enforce, in the course of a lawsuit, the claim in favour of the company, within 30 days from the date of the general meeting of members/partners.

(2) Omission of the term of indent (1) involves the loss of any such rights.

Managers

para. 197

(1) One or several managers elected for a fixed period of time should be in charge of management of matters of the limited liability company and should represent the company. The manager or managers should be elected from the members/partners (respectively their representatives) or of other natural persons, i.e. not members to the company. The deed of association may also provide that all members/partners (representatives) should be entitled to management and representation; In this case, these persons should be considered as managers.

(2) The first managers should be appointed in the deed of association. The deed of association may not legally deviate from this provision.

(3) If the limited liability company has several managers, these shall be entitled solely to joint representation, unless the deed of association provides otherwise. If a declaration has to be made to the company proper, even one manager is sufficient.

para. 198

In the case of a one-man limited liability company – if the founder is a nantural person – the foundation deed may also provide that the founder shall be entitled to both management and representation. In such a case, the founder shall be considered as manager.

para. 199

(1) The manager shall represent the limited liability company in relation to any third persons, as well as at Courts and other authorities. The manager may invest his above outlined sphere of authority even to employees of the limited liability company, concerning certain defined groups of matters.

(2) The deed of association may limit the right of representation of the manager; Any such limitation should, however, be considered as ineffective towards any third persons.

(3) The manager, respectively in the case of several managers, the appointed manager shall exercise the employer's rights with respect to employees/workers of the limited liability company.

para. 200

(1) Unless the general meeting of members/partners has agreed, the manager may not:
(a) Carry on in his own name any businesslike business activity within the scope of activities of the limited liability company;
(b) Be a member of unlimited responsibility of another business company engaging in activities similar to that of the said limited liability company;
(c) Be a leading officer of any other business society, association, company or venture carrying on activities similar to those of the limited liability company.

(2) Should the manager infringe any of the prohibitions which indent (1) defines, the limited liability company may

(a) require indemnification;

(b) instead of indemnification, it may require the manager to transfer the business transaction he has concluded in his own favour to the limited liability company or

(c) the manager should abandon his profit from the business transaction he concluded on behalf of or on account of another person or company or should assign his demands ensuing from the said transaction to the limited liability company.

(3) The claim as per indent (2) of the limited liability company is statutorily limited to 3 months after the day the managers (in the case of a single manager, the members or partners of the limited liability company) have taken notice of any vent of indent (2). After the elapse of one year from the day of occurrence of the claim, same cannot anymore be enforced.

para. 201

(1) The managers shall have to keep records on the members/partners of the limited liability company (list of members/partners).

(2) The following data shall have to be indicated in the list of members/partners:

(a) The name (company), address (seat) and the basic deposit of each member/partner,

(b) the provisions of the deed of association concerning any possible additional payments to be made and secondary services as well as the rights of preemption the members/partners may exercise,

(c) all changes taking place in persons (entities) of members/partners, respectively in their respective shares in the company, thus e.g. the transfer of business shares, the division of same, the purchase of such business shares or cancellation by the limited liability company.

(3) The manager shall have to report the data the list of members contains and any changes taking place in the said list to the Court of Registration, for entry.

(4) Anybody who can prove the probability of his interest, may inspect the list of members/partners.

para. 202

(1) The managers shall have to take measures for the regular keping of the business-books of the limited liability company.

(2) The managers shall have to draw the balance-sheet of the limited liability company as well as prepare the inventory of its property/assets and shall have to submit these to the general meeting of members/partners.

para. 203

(1) At members'/partners' demand, the managers shall have to supply informa-

tion on the matters of the limited liability company and shall have to enable the inspection of the business books and documents of the company.

(2) Should the managers fail to comply with this demand, the member concerned may file a petition with the Court of Registration. The Court of Registration shall immediately pass an executable decision – beyond any lawsuit –after consulting the involved parties. No appeal can be lodged against the Court's decision.

para. 204

The managers shall jointly and severally be responsible with the limited liability company in respect of any third persons for the falsity of data submitted to the Court of Registration.

para. 205

(1) A decision passed with a majority of three quarter parts of votes of the general meeting of members/partners is necessary for recalling the managers.

(2) Any changes taking place in the persons of managers or their rights of representation shall have to be reported to the Court of Registration for entry and publication.

para. 206

(1) Should the number of managers of the limited liability company drop below the number the deed of association has defined, the managers shall have to convoke the general meeting of members/partners within 30 days.

(2) If no manager of the limited liability company has been left, the Court of Registration shall convoke the general meeting of members/partners upon request of any of the interested parties.

para. 207

The limited liability company shall be responsible for the damage its managers have caused to any third person by their activities falling within their scope of activities.

Supervisory Board

para. 208

(1) If the number of members/partners of the limited liability company, the significance or character if its activity justifies, the deed of association may form a Supervisory Board consisting of not less than 3 members.

(2) Formation of the Supervisory Board is mandatory in the following cases:
(a) If the basic capital of the limited liability company surpasses 20 million Forint, or

(b) if the number of members/partners of the limited liability company surpasses 25 or

(c) if the number of the full-time employees/workers of the limited liability company is more than 200 heads on the annual average.

(3) As regards a one-man limited liability company, organization of the Supervisory Board shall be mandatory solely in the case as point (c) of indent (2) provides.

para. 209

(1) The general meeting of members/partners shall elect the members of the Supervisory Board, except for the case para. 210 regulates.

(2) The general meeting of members/partners may not elect any employee of the limited liability company to a member of the Supervisory Board.

(3) A majority of at least three quarter parts of votes is necessary for recalling a member of the Supervisory Board whom the general meeting of members/partners has elected; The deed of association may legally not deviate from this provision.

para. 210

(1) If organization of a Supervisory Board is mandatory – except for the case which point (c) of indent (2) of para. 208 has mentioned – the deed of association shall have to appoint the first Supervisory Board.

The deed of association may legally not deviate from this provision.

(2) If in the Supervisory Board formed in compliance with point (c) of indent (2) of para. 208 the opinion of the representatives of employees/workers differ from that of the Supervisory Board, the opinion of the said minority shall have to be expounded on as well at the general meeting of members/partners.

para. 211

The members of the Supervisory Board can be present and can rise to speak at the general meeting of members/partners.

para. 212

The Supervisory Board shall compulsorily convoke the general meeting of partners/members if the managers have omitted to do so or if the interests of the company otherwise require such a meeting.

para. 213

An appointed member of the Supervisory Board shall represent the limited liabililty company in the management by the managers and furthermore in lawsuits filed against the managers.

para. 214

The provisions of para. 200 shall apply also to the members of the Supervisory Board.

The auditor

para. 215

Appointment of an auditor is mandatory in the case of a one-man limited liability company.

Amendment of the deed of association

para. 216

(1) A decision passed by at least a majority of three quarter parts of votes of the general meeting of partners/members shall be necessary for amending the deed of association.

(2) The unanimous decision by the general meeting of partners/members would be necessary for increasing the liabilities of members/partners the deed of association has stipulated, for defining new liabilities, duties, respectively for jeopardizing the extra rights of certain members/partners.

(3) The deed of association may legally not deviate from the provisions of indents (1) and (2).

para. 217

Any amendment of the deed of association shall have to be reported jointly by all managers to the Court of Registration for entry and publishing

Raising the base capital

para. 218

(1) If the general meeting of partners/members has decided in favour of increasing the base capital, the raised base capital shall have to be covered by paying in new basic deposits (respectively by supplying them), except for the exception of para. 221.

(2) Unless all former basic deposits have fully been paid up, the base capital may not be raised.

(3) The decision stating the raising of the base capital shall have to be reported jointly by all managers to the Court of Registration, for entry and publication.

para. 219

(1) Members/partners of the limited liability company who have been entered in

the Register before raising the base capital shall have a right of preemption concerning the new basic deposits, within 30 days from entering the decision, stating the raising of the base capital into the log of decisions. The members/partners can exercise their rights of preemption in proportion to their basic deposits.

(2) If the members/partners have not exercised their rights of preemption within the specified term, the persons (entities) appointed by them are entitled to acquire the new basic deposits or in lack of such appointed persons or entities, anybody may acquire the new basic deposits.

(3) A statement made in the form of an official/notarial document or deed or a private deed signed by the person/entity acquiring the new basic deposit of probative force shall be required for acquiring a new basic deposit. Any possibly undertaken secondary services shall have to be indicated in the statement, respectively, the person or entity acquiring the new basic deposit shall have to state that he/it recognizes the provisions of the deed of association as mandatory for himself/itself.

(4) The general meeting of members/partners shall decide on accepting the statement; Upon accepting the statement, the person or legal entity making the statement shall become a member/partner of the limited liability company, without any separate amendment of the deed of association.

para. 220

(1) The provisions concerning the minimum sum of the basic deposit, on the method of payment, term and legal consequences of delay shall apply also in connection with the new basic deposits.

(2) If the new basic deposit is supplied in kind (i.e. not in the form of money), the rules concerning evaluation of the deposit and the responsibility of the member/partner supplying the deposit shall be applicable also to the new basic deposits.

para. 221

The general meeting of members/partners may even rule that the base capital should be raised from assets of the company over and above the base capital. Such an increase in the base capital will increase the basic deposits by members/partners without making any separate payment, in proportion with the former basic deposits.

para. 222

(1) The fact of raising the base capital shall be reported jointly and severally by all managers to the Court of Registration, for entry and publication. Unless at least one half of all basic deposits have been paid up, respectively the basic deposits in kind have been fully made available to the limited liability company, the entry by the Court of Registration cannot take place.

(2) The raising of the base capital becomes valid by its entry in the Trade Register.

para. 223

If the one-man limited liability company becomes completed by new members/ partners on account of dividing the business shares or raising the base capital, the company shall be bound to transform itself into a limited liability company in compliance with the general rules and regulations. The transformation shall have to be reported to the Court of Registration by all managers jointly and severally, for entry and publication.

Decreasing the base capital

para. 224

(1) The base capital may not be reduced to a sum lower than Ft. 1 million. If reduction of the base capital takes places by refunding a certain part of the basic deposits, the minimum sum of the residual basic deposits may not be less than Ft. 100 000.

(2) All managers shall have to jointly report the decision by the general meeting of partners/members on reducing the base capital to the Court of Registration, for entry and publication.

para. 225

(1) After having duly reported on the decision stating the reduction of the base capital to the Court of Registration, the managers shall have to publish twice the respective announcement at an interval of 30 days in the Official Gazette. The announcement shall expound on the decision stating the reduction of the base capital and the creditors of the limited liability company shall simultaneously be summoned to give notice of their claims within 3 months from the last publication of the announcement. Any known creditors shall even separately be summoned to report their claims.

(2) The demands of creditors who have reported their claims within the above term to the limited liability company and who have refused to agree in decreasing the base capital shall have to be paid up or they should be supplied with security.

para. 226

(1) Before the elapse of the term indent (1) of para. 225 specifies, all managers shall have to report to the Court of Registration that the demands of creditors who have failed to agree with decreasing the base capital have been supplied, i.e. paid up, respectively that they have been given securities. Copies of the Offical Gazette containing the announcements shall have to be enclosed in the said report.

(2) Decreasing of the base capital can be entered only after the report of indent (1). The decrease of the base capital becomes valid only upon the entry.

(3) Repayments to members/partners based on decreasing the base capital may be made solely after entry of reducing the base capital into the Trade Register.

Winding-up the company

para.227

A decision passed by a majority of at least three quarter parts of the general meeting of members/partners is necessary for deciding the winding-up of the limited liability company. The deed of association may not legally deviate from this provision.

para. 228

If the limited liability company is winding up without any legal successor, the rules concerning final accounting shall be applicable with the complements of paras. 229 and 230.

para. 229

The meeting of members/partners shall decide, simultaneously with approving the closing balance-sheet, on the acquittal of officers in charge of final accounting (the managers), the auditors and the Supervisory Board.

para. 230

(1) From the assets remaining after paying off the creditors, the additional payments by partners/members shall be refunded first, and the residual portion shall have to be distributed among the members/partners of the limited liability company in proportion with their basic deposits.

(2) It is prohibited to distribute the assets before 6 months have elapsed after having published the summons to creditors for the third time in the Official Gazette.

para. 231

If the number of members/partners of the limited liability company drops to one, and the company does not report to the Court of Registration a new member within 6 months, the limited liability company does not cease to exist (it is not wound-up) but continues its operation as a one-man limited liability company, by applying the relevant rules and regulation. All managers shall have to report this circunstance to the Court of Registration for entry and publication.

Chapter VII. Share company (Joint stock company, stock corporation, company limited by shares)

General rules

para. 232

(1) The share company (joint stock company, stock corporation, company limit-

ed by shares) is a business society, association, company or venture which is founded with a registered capital (capital stock share capital) comprising shares of predetermined nominal values; The responsibility of shareholders (members) towards the company covers the supply of the value of issue or the nominal value of the share. The shareholder is otherwise not responsible for any liabilities of the company limited by shares.

(2) The title: company limited (limited company, company limited shares, share company etc) or its abbreviation 'rt' (in Hungarian language) must be indicated in the firm name of the company.

para. 233

Unless the present Law so provides, any deviations from the rules and regulations concerning the limited company would be impermissible. Any contrary legal statement should be considered as null and void.

The share

para. 234

(1) The share is a security or bond embodying membership rights (within the company).

(2) Each share provides identical membership rights (in the company). Shares providing membership rights other than those which the statutes of the association (company) define can, however, be issued based on a law or on legal authorization.

(3) Shares providing identical membership rights represent a kind of share (paras. 242 through 245). The rights attached to a kind of share, as well as the number and the nominal value of shares to be issued of each, and one kind of share shall have to be stated in the statutes of association. The shares belonging to a certain kind of shares shall have identical nominal (face) values.

para. 235

(1) The nominal or face value of a share shall be not less than Ft 10 000 or a multiple of this amount provided it is divisible with 10 000 without any residue.

(2) The issue of shares below the nominal or face value shall be considered as null and void; The issuers or floaters shall jointly and severally be responsible for any damages resulting from issuing such shares.

(3) The sum of the nominal or face values of the totality of shares is the registered or stock capital of the limited company.

para. 236

Shares shall be printed by a printing office, by complying with the rules and regulations concerning securities (bonds). This rule shall apply also to shares certificates or warrants and interim shares.

para. 237

The following minimum data shall be shown on the share:
(a) The firm name and seat (headquarters) of the limited company;
(b) The serial number, nominal (face) value of the share and it should also be indicated whether the share is a bearer's share or a registered share and in case of a registered share the owner's name shall be indicated as well:
(c) The kind of share and the rights attached to it as the statutes define;
(d) The date of issue, the amount of the registered capital upon issue and the number of shares;
(e) The signature of the Board of Directors, in compliance with the rules for signing for the limited company;
(f) In the case of a share certificate and an interim share, the already paid-up sum.

para. 238

(1) Any shares issued before entering the limited company in the Trade Register and before paying in full the registered capital shall be considered as null and void, but until entering the limited company into the Trade Register, a share certificate can be issued on the paid-up part of the registered capital.

(2) After having registered the limited company into the Trade Register, interim shares can be issued on the registered capital paid up in part.

(3) The share certificate and the interim share are registered and the sum paid by the shareholder up to issuing the said securities should be shown on the latter. The issuers, floaters, respectively the members of the Board of Directors shall be jointly and severally responsible for any damage which infringing of this rule may cause.

para. 239

The shareholder may require the handing over of shares due to him after entry of the limited company in the Trade Register and after paying up in full the registered capital.

para. 240

(1) Bearer shares can be freely transferred.

(2) The rules concerning endorsing bills of exchange shall be applicable to the transference of registered shares, with the limitation, however that the transference of the share comes into force with respect to the limited company if the name of the new owner is already figuring in the Book of Shares.

(3) Foreigners can acquire solely registered shares. In the case of an inheritance, the bearer share of a foreigner shall have to be converted into a registered share within one year from the transfer of the bequest or inheritance.

para. 241

(1) The Board of Directors of the limited company shall keep a Book of Shares

on the registered shares and shall keep evidence in the said book of the name (firm) and address (seat) of shareholders.

(2) On making entries into the Book of Shares, the limited company is not required to check the statement of transfer for authenticity.

(3) The shareholder may demand a copy of the part relating to himself of the Book of Shares from the Board of Directors.

para. 242

(1) In accordance with the rules of Statutes, the limited company may issue shares entitling the bearer of the share to a dividend preceding any other kinds of shares of obtaining dividends from the profits divisible among the shareholders (priority share). The statutes of the company may limit or exclude the right of voting attached to the priority share.

(2) The statutes of the company shall define the rules for priority concering dividends.

(3) The statutes of the limited company can enable the issue of other kinds of priority shares as well.

(4) Priority shares can be issued up to and not exceeding one half of the registered capital of the limited company.

para. 243

(1) The statutes of the limited company may enable the issue of such registered shares which, after a period the statutes define, pass into the ownership of a foundation or association founded for some public objective. In the said case, a sum corresponding to the nominal or face value is due to the abandonee organization; the difference between the nominal (face) value and the current price value shall be due to the shareholder. Before the elapse of the period the statutes of the limited company define, all shareholders' rights are fully due to the shareholder.

(2) Should the limited company wind up without any successor before the time indent (1) defines the proportion in ratio with time of the face value of shares, but at least an annual 5%, shall have to be paid to the abandonee organization of indent (1).

(3) If the members of the abandonee organization of indent (1) are full-time workers or employees of the limited company, the statutes of the company may specify, provided the number of workers/employees is more than 50, then the actual dividends or a part of them after the said shares shall be due to the said organization (employee's foundation or association) subject to the conditions which the statutes of the company define. The pertinent rules of the statutes of the limited company may not be amended to the detriment of the abandonee organization; In the case of raising the registered capital, the said organization shall have the right of preemption concerning a part of the registered capital the statutes of the company have defined, but at least up to 10% of the registered capital.

para. 244

(1) Employees' shares available to employees free of any charge or at reduced prices can also be issued, corresponding to the rules of the statutes of the limited company. Such shares can be issued only from the assets over and above the registered capital of the limited company, along with simultaneously raising the registered capital and up to but not more than 10% of the raised registered capital.

(2) Employees' shares shall be registered shares which shall be transferable among the workers/employees and retired workers and employees of the limited company, by complying with the rules concerning the transference of registered shares.

(3) Upon the decease of the worker/employee or upon terminating his work relations with the limited company – except for the case of retirement – the limited company shall be due to purchase the employees' shares. The limited company shall have to purchase the share at the commercial value and at least at the face (nominal) value.

(4) The owners of employees' shares may exercise the same shareholders' rights as the other shareholders. The detailed conditions of acquiring and transferring (endorsing) such shares shall be defined by the Board of Directors and the Board may even enable that certain predefined groups of workers/employees may even jointly acquire such shares.

para. 245

(1) In accordance with the rules of the statutes of the limited company, shares entitling the owners to interest of a predetermined value can be issued to an extent not exceeding 10% of the registered capital.

(2) The owners of interest-bearing shares are due to interest calculated at the rate of interest shown on the share after the nominal/face value of the share, even if the limited company does not gain any profits in the given year.

(3) In addition to the interest, the owner of the interest-bearing share shall also be due to other rights attached to the share, including too the title of obtaining the dividend.

para. 246

(1) Up to one half of the registered capital, the limited company can issue bonds which can be converted, by the bearer, on demand, into a share (convertible bond).

(2) The limited company can decide to float even such bonds which upon raising the registered capital ensure preemption rights for new shares to be issued later by the limited company (bonds warranting preemption right).

(3) The rules and regulations for the convertible bond and the bond providing preemption right shall be defined by the statutes of the limited company.

para. 247

(1) The limited company may acquire from the assets it owns, beyond the registered capital its own, already fully paid-up shares.

(2) The sum of the total nominal (face) value of private shares in the ownership of the limited company may not surpass one third part of the registered capital.

(3) Based on the private shares it acquires, the limited company may not exercise any shareholders' rights – unless the present Law provides otherwise – and shall be compelled to sell such shares within 3 years.

para. 248

(1) The limited company may redeem (cancel) the private shares it has acquired. This method of redeeming or cancelling shares will not reduce the sum of the registered capital.

(2) Redeemed, cancelled registered shares shall have to be deleted in the Book of Shares and both the registers, and the bearer shares which have been redeemed or cancelled shall have to be annihilated.

(3) The Board of Directors shall have to report the redemption or cancellation of shares within 30 days to the Court of Registration for entry.

para. 249

(1) A share may even have several owners who, from the aspect of the limited company shall be considered as a single shareholder. Such owners may exercise their rights solely by way of a joint representative and shall be jointly responsible for any liabilities of shareholders.

(2) If a registered share is in joint ownership, the joint representative's name shall also have to be entered in the Book of Shares.

Foundation of a limited company

para. 250

The founder of a limited company is the issuer (emitter) of the draft of foundation. A limited company may even have a single founder.

para. 251

(1) The registered capital of a limited company may not be less than Ft. 10 million.

(2) The contribution in terms of money on foundation of the limited company may not be less than 30% of the registered capital and/or Ft. 5 million

Subcription for shares

para. 252

(1) The method of covering the registered capital of the limited company is the subscription for shares.

(2) The basis for subscription is the draft of foundation. The original copy of the foundation draft shall be entered in an official/notary document/deed or a private deed of full proving force, and the copies made of the document or deed shall have to be certified by a public notary.

(3) The following data shall have to be indicated in the draft of foundation:

(a) The firm name and seat (headquarters), sphere of activities, period of duration of the limited company;

(b) The planned amount of the registered capital;

(c) The number and nominal (face) value, respectively value as issued of shares; If various kinds of shares are issued, their designations and the rights they afford to shareholders;

(d) The place, the first and last day of subscribing shares;

(e) Advantages due to founders, thus particularly the right according to which they can appoint the members of the Board of Directors for the first 3 years;

(f) The subject value of contribution in kind and the number of shares to be given as a countervalue for such contribution in kind, the name (firm), place of dwelling (seat or headquarters) of the person (society, association, company, venture) providing the contribution and the name (firm) of the auditor in charge of the preliminary evaluation;

(g) The procedure to be followed in case of over-subscribing;

(h) The method of convoking the foundation general assembly.

para. 253

(1) The founders shall have to indicate in the form of a written statement the data according to which they have defined the value of any contribution of non-financial character, i.e. contribution in kind.

(2) The draft foundation may consider the value of the contribution in kind at a value not higher than that which the auditor has previously defined.

para. 254

(1) Subscription for shares shall take place by signing the subscription form. Shares can be subscribed for either in person or by a representative.

(2) The subscriber for shares shall have to transfer at least 10% of the sum he has subscribed to the banker's account the founders have determined except for the case when the subscriber intends to supply a contribution in kind.

para. 255

(1) If more shares have been subscribed for than the limited company would

issue according to the draft foundation (over-subscribing), the founders may reject the over-subscription. Unless such a rejection has been stated, the foundation general assembly shall decide on accepting or rejecting the excess subscription in the course of eventually defining the registered capital.

(2) Subscription of shares by a state budgetary organ or a banking institute may not be rejected.

(3) If the founders or the foundation general assembly have rejected the over-subscription, the value of the excess subscription shall have to be refunded without any reduction to the subscribers for shares within 15 days after the rejection. The founders shall jointly be responsible for complying with this liability.

para. 256

(1) Foundation of the limited company shall be considered as a failure if shares of a sum corresponding to the full planned registered capital of the limited company have not been subscribed for.

(2) In case of failure of subscribing, any sum deposited or transferred by the subscribers for shares shall have to be refunded without any deduction within 15 days. The founders shall jointly be responsible for compliance with this liability.

Foundation general assembly

para. 257

(1) The founders shall have to convoke the foundation general assembly within 60 days from the last day of the successful subscription for shares.

(2) Should the founders omit to convoke the foundation general assembly within the term as indent (1) specified, subscribers for shares are considered to be relieved from their liabilities and may require repayment of the sum they have deposited, i.e. paid. The founders shall jointly be responsible for effecting the repayment without deduction.

(3) Before opening the foundation general assembly, the share–subscriber shall have to complement the sum he has paid upon subscription up to 30% of the nominal (face) value of the shares he has subscribed for. This provision does not apply to a subscriber who has undertaken to supply contribution in kind.

para. 258

The foundation general assembly (the statutory general meeting) shall
(a) State that the registered capital has been subscribed for and that at least 30% of the registered capital has been paid for;
(b) Accept or reject any over-subscription;
(c) Decide on the foundation of the limited company;
(d) Define the Statutes;
(e) Decide on advantages due to founders and on the approval of any separate agreements which have been made with the founders or others in the course of foundation;

(f) Decide on the approval of contracts which have been concluded up to the date of the foundation general assembly (statutory meeting);

(g) Decide on the value of any contributions in kind and on the term of supplying such contribution;

(h) Elect the Board of Directors and the Supervisory Board for the first year of operation except in the case where the founders have preserved this right for themselves in the draft foundation;

(i) Elect the auditor of the limited company.

para. 259

(1) The foundation general meeting (statutory meeting) has a quorum when at least five share-subscribers are present, either in person or by representatives, having written authorizations who have subscribed for at least one half of the registered capital.

(2) The foundation general meeting shall make decisions by the simple majority of votes but may deviate from the draft foundation only by a unanimous decision of all subscribers for shares and may not define the value of the contribution in kind at a value higher than the draft foundation or the auditor has determined, and may not alter the advantages due to the founders to the burden of the limited company.

(3) The interested subscribers for shares may not vote when deciding on the contribution in kind and the advantages due to the founders.

(4) Records shall be kept on the foundation general assembly (statutory meeting).

Exclusive foundation

para. 260

(1) If the founders have agreed in a foundation deed countersigned by an attorney or legal adviser that they take over all shares at proportions they have themselves defined, it is unnecessary to issue a draft foundation and the subscription for shares and the foundation general assembly (statutory meeting) are superfluous.

(2) In the case of an exclusive foundation, the founders shall appoint the members of the Board of Directors and the Supervisory Board.

(3) The general provisions concerning foundation shall apply, according to the meaning, to questions which indents (1) and (2) have not regulated.

(4) A limited company cannot be founded by exclusive foundation if the founders are exclusively natural persons.

Articles

para. 261

(1) The Articles shall define the following:

(a) The firm name and seat (headquarters) of the limited company;

140

(b) The duration of the limited company;

(c) The sphere of activity of the limited company;

(d) The size (value) of the registered capital, the conditions of paying for the shares;

(e) The number, nominal (face) value of shares and whether the shares will be bearer shares or registered shares;

(f) The method of signing for the limited company;

(g) The method of convoking the general assembly, the necessary quorum, the mode of procedure whenever the general assembly would have no quorum, the preconditions for exercising the right of voting and the method of exercising the right of voting;

(h) The number of members of the Board of Directors and the Supervisory Board as well as of auditors, the mode of electing them, their spheres of activities and the duration of their operation;

(i) The rules for distributing the profit;

(j) The mode of making known (publishing) the announcements of the limited company;

(k) The consequences of omitting the settlement (paying-up for shares).

(2) The Articles shall provide, as necessary, for the following:

(a) Any separate agreements concerning deposits (contributions) in kind and other advantages possibly warranted for founders;

(b) If various kinds of shares have been issued, on designation, number, nominal (face) value and attached rights of such shares;

(c) If convertible bonds or bonds ensuring preemption rights are issued, on the relevant rules;

(d) The possibility of cancelling (withdrawing) shares and the procedure to be followed in such cases;

(e) On raising the registered capital, the preconditions for the authorization given to the Board of Directors (para. 306);

(f) On everything the shareholders wish to include into the Articles.

Reporting the limited company to the Court of Registration

para. 262

(1) The foundation of the limited company shall be reported to the Court of Registration for entry and publishing. The members of the Board of Directors of the limited company shall have to jointly submit this report.

(2) The limited company may be entered in the Trade Register solely upon proving that:

(a) the convoking of the foundation general assembly has taken place regularly,

(b) the subscribers for shares have subscribed for the entire registered capital,

(c) at least 30% of the registered capital has in fact been paid up.

para. 263

Before the entry of the limited company in the Trade Register has taken place, the subscriber for shares cannot transfer the rights he has gained by signing the form of subscription with a force affecting the limited company to any other person or entity.

Rights and liabilities of shareholders

para. 264

(1) Within one year taken from the entry of the limited company in the Trade Register, the shareholder shall have to pay up the full value of shares. Within the said term, he shall have to comply with the said liability as soon as the Board of Directors has made public the summons in accordance with the conditions the articles of the limited company have provided requiring the shareholders to make the said payment. The owners of registered shares shall also have to be summoned to pay up separately.

(2) Should the shareholder be late in paying up the money due to the subscribed shares, he shall be bound to pay an annual interest of 20%.

(3) Should the shareholder fail to comply with paying the due amount within 60 days from the date of summoning him, the Board of Directors shall be entitled to sell the interim share by way of public auction, by simultaneously cancelling it and abolishing the shareholder's rights. The received sum shall be used primarily for meeting the demand of the limited company in connection with the share while the residual part of the sum shall be due to the former shareholder.

para. 265

Should the shareholder transfer his interim certificate to any other person before paying up the full nominal (face) value, he shall be responsible for his liabilities as a guarantor.

para. 266

(1) The shareholder shall have a right to receive a proportional part (dividend) of the profits as per balance-sheet which the general assembly has ordered to distribute among the shareholders.

(2) Should the limited company wind-up without any legal successor, the shareholders shall have the right to obtain a part in proportion to his shares of the assets divisible as a result of final accounting.

(3) The provisions of indents (1) and (2) shall not affect any special rights which the articles define in respect of certain kinds of shares.

(4) Except for the case of decreasing the registered capital, it shall be prohibited to pay on the account of the registered capital any amounts to shareholders.

para. 267

(1) Neither during the existence of the limited company, nor upon its winding-

up may the shareholder require refunding of his contribution in kind he has executed.

(2) The shareholder cannot be compelled to refund any dividends he has taken receipt of in good faith.

para. 268

(1) Every shareholder shall be entitled to take part in the meeting of the general assembly, to ask for information and to make comments. Based on a share entitling him to vote, the shareholder shall have the right to make proposals and to vote.

(2) The Board of Directors shall be complied to supply the necessary information to every shareholder as regards matters on the general assembly, provided the shareholder has submitted in written form his respective request at least 8 days before the day of the general assembly. The Board of Directors may refuse the supply of such information solely if this would infringe some significant economic value or business secret of the limited company.

(3) The Board of Directors shall publish, according to the provisions of articles concerning publishing the announcements of the limited company the balance-sheet, the proposal on distribution of results (profits), as well as at least the essential data of the respective reports of the Board of Directors and the Supervisory Board at least 30 days before the meeting of the general assembly.

para. 269

(1) The right of voting attached to the share shall be adapted to the nominal (face) value of the share – except for the kind of share mentioned under para. 242.

(2) The articles may limit the exercise of the right of voting by determining the highest number of votes or ratios which the shares represent.

(3) The articles may enable a state budgetary order or a banking institute to exercise 51% of the rights of voting in possession of shares equal to not less than one third part of the registered capital.

para. 270

(1) The method of exercising the right of voting shall be determined by the articles.

(2) The shareholder may not exercise his right of voting until he has duly supplied due contribution in kind.

para. 271

(1) The shareholder may exercise his rights connecting the meeting of the general assembly even by way of a representative. Members of the Board of Directors, of the Supervisory Board and the auditor may not represent a shareholder in this context.

(2) The validity of the representative's authorization is valid for one meeting of the general assembly, including also the general assembly again convoked on

account of having no quorum. The authorization should be submitted to the limited company either in the form of an official/notarial document (deed) or a private document (deed) of probative force.

para. 272

Should the limited company fail to pay or pay, but not in full, the dividend warranted in favour of priority shares limiting or excluding the right of vote in one of the years, and if the limited company fails to make up for this non-payment in the next year jointly with the dividend due for the last mentioned year, then the priority shares shall obtain the right of voting and their holders may exercise this right until the limited company does not pay up the deferred dividend.

para. 273

(1) The general assembly shall be convoked if shareholders representing at least one tenth part of the registered capital demand in writing the Board of Directors to do so, by indicating the cause and the objective. The articles can provide this right even to shareholders representing a lower ratio of the registered capital.

(2) The Court of Registration shall convoke the general assembly if it has been requested to do so, in compliance with the provisions of indent (1), but the Board of Directors has failed to convoke the meeting within 30 days.

para. 274

(1) The shareholders having the right of vote representing at least one tenth part of the registered capital can request the Board of Directors, by indicating the cause and the objective, to set a question on the agenda of the general assembly. The articles may afford this right even to shareholders representing a smaller ratio of the registered capital.

(2) The shareholders may exercise their right as per indent (1) within 8 days from the date of publication of the announcement on convoking the general assembly.

(3) The Board of Directors shall be compelled to set the proposal as per indent (1) on the agenda of the general assembly and shall have to publish it within 8 days in a way similar to the announcement of the general assembly.

(4) Should the Board of Directors fail to comply with its liabilities which indent (3) has specified, the Court of Registration shall compensate for the failure upon request of the shareholders submitting the motion, within 3 days of submitting the respective demand.

para. 275

(1) The shareholders representing at least one tenth part of the registered capital may request, by indicating the cause, the Supervisory Board in writing to supervise the activities of the Board of Directors. The articles may also entitle

144

shareholders representing a lower ratio of the registered capital to exercise the above right.

(2) Should the Supervisory Board fail to comply with the motion of indent (1) within 30 days, the shareholders which indent (1) has stipulated may turn to the general assembly (para. 273).

para. 276

(1) The member of any of the Boards may demand the supervision by a Court of a decision infringing a law which the general assembly has taken.

(2) If the suit has been initiated by a member of the Board of Directors, the limited company shall be represented in the lawsuit by a member of the Supervisory Board appointed by the said Board. If a member of the Supervisory Board initiates the suit, the Court shall appoint a trustee (fiduciary) to the limited company.

(3) The shareholder initiating a suit shall have to deposit with the Court at least one of his shares.

(4) The provisions under Heading 4 of Chapter II shall otherwise apply to the supervision by Court of a decision infringing a law, according to the meaning, however, with the stipulation that the Court's decision shall cover also those shareholders who have not been parties to the lawsuit.

The organization of the limited company
The general assembly (meeting)

para. 277

The general assembly is the supreme organ of the limited company and comprises the totality of shareholders.

para. 278

The following actions shall be within the exclusive sphere of authority of the general assembly:
(a) Drafting and amending the articles;
(b) Raising and reducing the registered capital;
(c) Amending certain rights attached to various kinds of shares;
(d) Deciding on the association with, fusion, separation and winding-up of the limited company with some other limited company or on its conversion into another form of business society, association, company or venture;
(e) Election, revoking the members of the Board of Directors, the Supervisory Board – except for the case which para. 292 regulates – and the auditor, as well as defining their remunerations;
(f) Definition of the balance-sheet and distribution of the annual profits;
(g) Decisions on issuing convertible shares or shares providing preemption rights;
(h) Decisions on all questions which the Law or the articles have provided to be in the exclusive sphere of authority of the general assembly.

para. 279

(1) The general assembly shall be convened at the frequency as provided by the articles but at least once in a year. Whenever necessary, the general assembly can be convened at any time.

(2) The general assembly shall be convened by the Board of Directors unless the present Law has otherwise provided.

(3) Convocation of the general assembly shall have to be announced by the way the articles provide, at least 30 days before the first day of the meeting of the general assembly. The announcement shall contain the following:

(a) The firm name and seat (headquarters) of the limited company;

(b) The date and place of the general assembly;

(c) The conditions the articles have specified for exercising the right of voting.

(4) The owner of registered shares shall be notified also by a separate invitation on convening the general assembly.

para. 280

(1) An attendance sheet shall be prepared to register the shareholders present at the general assembly; The name (company) of the shareholder, respectively his representative, his address (seat, headquarters), the number of his shares and the number of votes to which the shares entitle him shall have to be indicated in the attendance sheet.

(2) The attendance sheet shall be certified by the signature of the general assembly and the person in charge of drawing up the records, or minutes.

para. 281

(1) If shareholders representing more than one half of the shares entitling their holders with the right of voting are present, the general assembly has a quorum; The articles may provide even a higher proportion of presence.

(2) If the general assembly has no quorum, a second general assembly which has been convened for a term within 15 days shall have a quorum on all matters on the original agenda irrespective of the number of shareholders there present.

(3) The general assembly may decide on matters not figuring in the published agenda only if all shareholders are present and if they unanimously agree on passing the said decision.

para. 282

In the matters listed under points (a) through (d) of para. 278, the general assembly decides by a majority of at least three quarter parts of the actual votes and on other matters by the simple majority of votes unless the articles specify some specific majority.

146

para. 283

Any decision of the general assembly that would unfavourably amend a right attached to a kind of share shall be only effective if at least a majority of three quarters shares representing the kind of share in question agree on the said amendment – by the way the articles specify or if the articles do not specify anyway by applying the rules and regulations concerning the general assembly.

para. 284

(1) Records or minutes shall be drawn up on the general assembly and this should contain the following:
(a) The firm name of the limited company and its seat (headquarters);
(b) The place and time of the general assembly;
(c) The names of the chairman of the general assembly, of the person in charge of drawing up the records, respectively minutes, of the persons in charge of certifying the records/minutes and the names of those canvassing the votes;
(d) The main events which have taken place in the course of the general assembly meeting and any motions, or proposals which have been submitted;
(e) The decisions, the number of votes for and against the decisions as well as the number of shareholders who have abstained from voting;
(f) The objection of a shareholder, a member of the Board of Directors or the Supervisory Board against some of the decisions, if the protesting person so desires.

(2) The records/minutes shall be signed by the person in charge of keeping the records/minutes and the chairman of the general assembly and shall have to be calibrated by two shareholders present at the general assembly and elected to do so.

(3) The Board of Directors shall have to submit a certified copy of the records/minutes of the general assembly, the sheet of attendance and the newspapers containing the announcement on convening the general assembly to the Court of Registration within 30 days after terminating the meeting of the general assembly.

(4) Any shareholder may request the Board of Directors to issue him an excerpt or a copy of the records/minutes of the general assembly.

The Board of Directors

para. 285

(1) The Board of Directors is the managing body of the limited company. This Board represents the limited company towards third persons, at Courts and other authorities; It organizes and controls the working organization of the limited company and exercises the employer's rights.

(2) The Board of Directors shall consist of at least 3 and not more than 11 members (directors). The Board shall elect its chairman among its own members.

(3) The directors shall be elected by the general assembly either from among the shareholders or others.

(4) Unless the articles provide otherwise, all directors shall jointly be entitled to manage the limited company.

para. 286

(1) Each director is entitled to sign for the firm of the limited company. The articles may, however require that several directors jointly or the Board of Directors jointly with an authorized person may sign for the firm.

(2) The articles may authorize certain directors out of the members of the Board of Directors or employees of the limited company to represent the limited company in general or certain defined matters.

para. 287

The articles, a decision of the general assembly or the Supervisory Board can limit the right of representation of the Board of Directors; Any such limitation would, however, be ineffective toward third persons. The members of the Board of Directors shall jointly be responsible to the limited company for any damage due to infringing this limitation.

para. 288

(1) Drawing up, working out the balance-sheet, respectively property assessment of the limited company shall be the duty of the Board of Directors; The proposal concerning division of profits shall similarly be the duty of the Board of Directors.

(2) The Board of Directors shall submit a report on the management, the property situation of the company and its business policy at the frequency which the articles specify but at least annually.

(3) The Board of Directors shall take care of the regular keeping of the business books of the limited company.

para. 289

The Board of Directors shall have to convene the meeting of the general assembly by also simultaneously notifying the Supervisory Board in the following cases:
(a) If the Board has noticed that the limited company has lost one third part of its registered capital or
(b) If the limited company has permanently stopped its payments or the assets of the company have not covered the debts.

para. 290

(1) A member of the Board of Directors may not:
(a) Conclude in his own name business transactions falling within the sphere of activity of the limited company;
(b) Be a member with unlimited responsibility of any other business society, asso-

ciation, company or venture conducting activities similar to that of the limited company;

(c) A leading official in another business society, association, company or venture carrying out activities similar to those of the limited company.

(2) Should a member of the Board of Directors infringe any of the prohibitions which indent (1) defines, the limited company shall be entitled to

(a) require indemnification,

(b) require, instead of indemnification, that the said member of the Board of Directors should transfer the business transaction he has concluded for his own purposes to the limited company or

(c) the said member of the Board of Directors shall transfer his profits from the business transaction he has concluded on his own account or should assign (make over) his claim concerning the said profit to the limited company.

(3) The demand as per indent (2) of the limited company shall be limited to three months from the date that the other members of the Board of Directors have noticed the activity or event as per indent (2). Any requirement or demand under this indent cannot be anymore enforced after the elapse of one year from its occurrence.

Supervisory Board

para. 291

(1) Every limited company is compelled to organize a Supervisory Board of at least 3 members.

(2) The general assembly shall elect the members of the Supervisory Board from the shareholders or others – except for the case which para. 292 regulates. The general assembly may not elect any worker/employee of the limited company as a member of the Supervisory Board.

para. 292

If the number of the full-time workers/employees of the limited company surpasses 200 on the annual average, one third part of the members of the Supervisory Board shall be elected by the workers/employees.

para. 293

(1) The members of the Supervisory Board shall participate in the meeting of the general assembly of the limited company; They may submit proposals concerning the agenda of the general assembly.

(2) Should the opinion of the representatives of workers'/employees' within the Supervisory Board differ from that of the Board, even this minority opinion should be expounded on before the general assembly.

149

para. 294

(1) The Supervisory Board may convene the general assembly if the interests of the limited company require this.

(2) In lawsuits initiated based on a decision of the general assembly against the Board of Directors or a member of the Board of Directors, the limited company shall be represented at Court by the Supervisory Board.

para. 295

(1) The Supervisory Board may exercise its rights either in a body (as a corporation) or by its members. The Board may even distribute its supervisory activities among its members, with a permanent character. The distribution of the supervisory activity does not affect the responsibility of the members of the Supervisory Board, neither their right to expand the supervisory activity even to other activities.

(2) If an internal superviser (supervisory organization) operates within the limited company, this internal superviser or the supervisory organization shall be controlled by the Supervisory Board.

para. 296

The provisions of para. 290 shall be applicable also to the members of the Supervisory Board.

Auditors

para. 297

(1) Each limited company shall have to elect at least one auditor.

(2) The auditor shall discharge the duties which the present Law or other legislative rules, the articles and the general assembly have stated for him to discharge.

One-man limited company

para. 298

(1) A limited company can be founded even so that the sole shareholder in it is a state budgetary organ or a banking institution.

(2) A one-man limited company also develops in the case when a single shareholder acquires the proprietary right of all shares. A natural person may not be a sole (one-man) shareholder.

para. 299

(1) The foundation (development) of a one-man limited company shall have to be reported within 30 days to the Court of Registration for entry in the Trade

Register and for publication. The responsibility of the shareholder of such a limited company for the liabilities of the said company will cover only the value of his shares.

(2) If the above said report is omitted, the shareholder shall be limited for all liabilities of the limited company without any limitation from the time all shares have been acquired by him.

(3) If on account of the permanent insolvency of the one-man limited company the winding-up procedure has to take place, the shareholder shall be responsible without any limit for all liabilities of the limited company which occurred after registering the one-man limited company into the Trade Register.

para. 300

The provisions concerning limited companies of this Law shall otherwise be applied to the one-man limited company, except for that the rights of the general assembly shall be exercised by the founder when indent (1) of para. 298 applies, respectively the shareholder if indent (2) of the said paragraph applies.

Increasing and decreasing the registered capital

Raising the registered capital

para. 301

(1) The limited company may raise its registered capital – except for the case which para. 304 regulates – provided the nominal (face) value of all earlier issued shares have been fully paid up. The articles of a bank, banking institution or insurance institute operating in the form of a limited company may even rule otherwise.

(2) Raising the registered capital can take place by subscribing for new shares, by converting the assets over and above the registered capital of the limited company into registered capital or by converting any convertible bonds into shares.

para. 302

(1) The general assembly shall decide on increasing the registered capital, upon a proposal submitted by the Board of Directors. In addition to those specified by indent (3) of para. 279, the following should be expounded in the announcement on convening the general assembly:
(a) the reasons, method and the minimum sum of increasing the registered capital,
(b) the draft of the modification of articles connected with increasing the registered capital,
(c) the number and value at issue of the new shares,
(d) if a new kind of share is issued, the rights attached to the new kind of share and whether the new share affects and in what method the rights attached to any earlier issued kinds of shares,

151

(e) if increasing the registered capital takes place by subscribing for shares, the first and last day of subscription,

(f) if increasing the capital takes place by contribution in kind, the proposal on this contribution.

(2) The practical implementation of increasing the registered capital is the duty of the Board of Directors.

para. 303

(1) If increasing the registered capital takes place by subscribing for shares,

(a) the sum which the general assembly has defined, but at least 30 % of the nominal (face) value of each share, shall have to be paid upon subscribing for the shares.

(b) by a three quarters majority of votes of shares entitling the shareholders the right of voting, the general assembly can provide a preemption right for every shareholder in proportion to their shares, by simultaneously determining the term within which the shareholders may exercise this one of their rights.

(2) Owners of bonds providing for the owners preemption right can exercise their right preceding that of the shareholders but the right of subscribing for shares of state budgetary organs, respectively banking institutions, precedes even the preemption right of owners of bonds.

(3) Otherwise, the rules for foundation as the present Law provides shall be applicable, according to the meaning, also to the subscription for shares in connection with increasing the registered capital,with the limitation, however, that the subscription for shares can be started only after registering and publishing the decision of the general assembly on the increase of the registered capital.

para. 304

(1) In case the increased portion of the registered capital is intended to be covered partly or fully by contributions in kind, the limited company can increase its registered capital with the value of the contribution in kind even if not all shares of the limited company have fully been paid up.

(2) The provisions concerning foundation of the Law shall apply, according to the meaning, for defining the value of the contribution in kind as well as the responsibility connected with the said contribution.

para. 305

(1) The limited company may incorporate any of its assets over and above the registered capital, respectively a part of such an asset in the registered capital by increasing the registered capital by increasing the registered capital of foundation – after accepting the annual or a separate, special balance-sheet – by issuing new shares or by overprinting (stamping) the previously printed shares.

(2) Unless the general assembly has otherwise decided, the new shares printed shall have to be offered for taking over – without demanding any countervalue – in proportion with the earlier shares owned by the shareholders. The pertinent sum-

mons should be published in the way the articles of the limited company have defined and the owners of registered shares shall also be given a separate notice of the place and term of taking over the new shares.

(3) If the shareholder fails to take receipt of the new shares up to terminating the next general assembly meeting, the limited company may sell the new shares.

(4) Overprinting (stamping) shall take place by indicating some higher nominal (face) value on the previously issued share, with full signatures in compliance with the provisions for signing the limited company.

para. 306

By simultaneously determining the pertinent conditions, the articles of the limited company can authorize the Board of Directors to increase the registered capital up to a defined sum in a way that the increase of the registered capital shall take place by issuing new shares equal to not more than one third part of the registered capital, or by converting the assets over and above the registered capital of the limited company into registered capital within not more than 5 years taken from the entry of the limited company in the Trade Register.

para. 307

(1) The general assembly can decide on a conditional increase of the registered capital if the objective of the said increase consists of issuing new convertible bonds.

(2) The owners of bonds may demand shares at the debit of the conditionally increased registered capital. The demand shall be submitted in written form and the number and nominal (face) value of the required shares shall be indicated simultaneously.

(3) The Board of Directors can issue shares solely for the purpose which the decision by the general assembly has provided, and after settling the full countervalue the decision has indicated, and to such an extent only to which the entitled persons have exercised their right to require new shares.

(4) If the Board of Directors has issued shares at a value lower than the nominal (face) value of shares, the new shares can only be drawn up if the entitled persons have already paid up the difference between the nominal (face) value of the share and the value embodied by the bond to the limited company; the shareholders' rights arise upon drawing up the share.

para. 308

(1) The decision on increasing the registered capital taken by the general assembly or the Board of Directors shall have to be reported by the Board of Directors to the Court of Registration within 30 days of passing the decision, for entry and publication. The same procedure shall apply after having implemented the increasing of the registered capital, respectively upon failure of the increase in the registered capital as well.

(2) In the case of a conditional increase in the registered capital, the Board of

Directors shall report within 30 days after approval of the balance-sheet to the Court of Registration – for entry in the Trade Register and publication – the increase in the registered capital which has taken place in the former year due to a conditional increase in the registered capital.

(3) The increase in the registered capital shall be valid from the day on which the Court of Registration has entered the increase of the registered capital in the Trade Register. The rules concerning foundation shall apply, according to the meaning, to the entry in the Trade Register.

(4) The shares (interim certificates) can be issued solely after the entry in the Trade Register; Any previous issue of shares shall be considered as null and void.

para. 309

(1) The new shares issued for increasing the registered capital – concerning the decision of the articles or the general assembly,- shall participate in the profits of the year during which the increase in registered capital has taken place.

(2) Shares in the private proprietary ownership of the limited company participate in increasing the registered capital according to the rules concerning the other shares.

Decreasing the registered capital

para. 310

(1) The reason, method of decreasing the registered capital and the sum by which the registered capital decreases along with the term up to which the shares have to be submitted to the limited company shall have to be defined in the decision of the general assembly on decreasing the registered capital.

(2) For decreasing the registered capital, first of all the private shares in the proprietary ownership of the limited company shall be involved.

(3) The rules concerning the minimum sum of the nominal (face) value of shares and the registered capital shall be complied with also upon decreasing the registered capital and any such decrease may not affect the rights of owners of convertible bonds.

para. 311

(1) The Board of Directors shall have to report the general assembly's decision on decreasing the registered capital to the Court of Registration for entry within 30 days from making the decision.

(2) Subsequent to reporting to the Court of Registration, the Board of Directors shall twice, consecutively, at intervals of not less than 30 days, publish the decision in the Official Gazette.

para. 312

(1) The creditors, whose claims are not yet due so far which have arisen against

the limited company before the first publication of the decision on decreasing the registered capital, may require from the limited company a security up to the sum of their claim within 90 days after the last publication of the decision on decreasing the registered capital. Omission of this term would involve the loss of rights.

(2) The limited company shall have to provide a security for creditors submitting their claims according to indent(1).

para. 313

The decrease of the registered capital may take place
(a) by exchanging, overprinting (stamping) the share or by reducing the number of shares by some similar method (fusion of shares) or
(b) by withdrawing, cancelling shares and by refunding any payments made after the shares to the shareholders.

para. 314

(1) Based on the decision of the general assembly, the limited company shall have to summon by an announcement that it has made public the shareholders to submit their shares for exchange, overprinting, withdrawal (cancellation) or fusion of shares. The limited company shall declare the shares which have not been submitted to it, in spite of the summons, as cancelled and invalid.

(2) The limited company shall publish in the Official Gazette the cancellation (withdrawal) of shares. In place of the cancelled (withdrawn) shares, the limited company may issue new shares and can sell the new shares and hand over, i.e. transfer the sales receipts to the interested parties or can deposit the sales receipts until establishing the title to the deposit.

para. 315

(1) Decreasing the registered capital by withdrawing (cancelling) shares may take place solely in the case of the articles expressively permitting such an action. The detailed rules of withdrawing (cancelling) shares shall be defined by the general assembly.

(2) Shares can be withdrawn (cancelled) by drawing lots and only if the provision permitting withdrawal (cancellation) has already been contained in the articles upon issuing the share intended to be withdrawn (cancelled).

para. 316

(1) After the elapse of 90 days taken from the last publication according to indent (2) of para. 311, the Court of Registration shall enter, at the limited company's demand, the decrease in the registered capital. The decrease in the registered capital comes into force by entering the decrease in the Trade Register.

(2) The entry can take place solely upon proving
(a) that the decision of the general assembly on decreasing the registered capital has twice taken place and

155

(b) the security which para. 312 specifies has been given or the creditors' claims have been fulfilled.

(3) Any payments to the shareholder to the debit of the registered capital can be made or any deferred payment for the share of the shareholder can be cancelled only after the decrease of the registered capital has been entered in the Trade Register.

Winding-up the limited company

para. 317

If winding-up the limited company without any legal successor, the provisions concerning final accounting shall be applicable with the completions of paras. 318— 320.

para. 318

(1) The duties concerning final accounting can even be transferred by the general assembly from the Directors to other person(s).

(2) Shareholders representing at least one tenth part of the registered capital or creditors may request, by indicating the reasons, the Court of Registration to appoint another person for final accounting. The articles can afford this right even to shareholders representing a smaller proportion of the registered capital.

para. 319

(1) Along with approving the closing balance-sheet, the general assembly shall decide on relieving the persons in charge of final accounting, the Board of Directors, the Supervisory Board and the auditor.

(2) The persons in charge of final accounting can request the shareholders to pay up any due payments, if the sums in question are necessary for settling the debts of the limited company or for covering the cost of final accounting or for some other reason.

para. 320

(1) The residual assets remaining after settling the debts shall be divided among the shareholders in proportion with their shares. If the limited company has also issued kinds of shares providing their shareholders with separate (special) rights, the said rights shall have to be taken into consideration on dividing (distributing) the assets.

(2) If the shareholders have made unequal payments for their shares, firstly the already effected payments shall be refunded; Any divisible assets remaining after this refund shall be distributed (divided) in proportion with the shares. If the assets to be distributed (divided) do not cover the refunding of already made payments, the deficit shall have to be made up by the shareholders in proportion with their shares.

(3) Until the elapse of 6 months following the publication of the summons to creditors printed for the third time in the Official Gazette, the assets may not be distributed.

Participation in other limited companies

para. 321

By acquiring shares, the limited company can acquire influence in other limited companies, by a significant participation, a majority participation or a mutual participation.

para. 322

(1) A significant participation is constituted by the fact that if the limited company has acquired shares amounting to more than one quarter of the registered capital of another limited company or if more than one quarter of the votes are due to the limited company at the general assembly of another limited company, provided that the participation so acquired does not qualify as a majority participation.

(2) The limited company acquiring the significant participation shall have to notify of this fact the other limited company without any delay and shall publish this fact also in the Official Gazette, by indicating the proportions of the acquired shares, respectively votes.

(3) If the limited company acquires a significant participation in another limited company and fails to comply with its liability as per indent (2), it may not exercise its shareholders' rights in the other limited company until it has met the said liability.

para. 323

(1) A majority participation shall be understood as follows: If a limited company has acquired the shares corresponding to more than one half of the registered capital of another limited company (controlled limited company) or if more than one half of the votes on the general assembly of another limited company are due to it, the participation shall be termed as a majority participation.

(2) For acquiring the majority participation, the other limited company shall be notified of this intention and a proposal shall have to be made to the shareholders of the limited company to be controlled concerning the planned purchase of shares, in order to acquire the majority participation. The purchasing tender shall contain the type, number and purchase price of shares intended to be purchased as well as the term of validity of the tender.

(3) The notification (announcement) and the tender for purchase shall have to be communicated in the Official Gazette; Publication of the tender shall qualify, according to indent (2) of para. 322 as sale as well. Shares based on the tender may be purchased solely 30 days after the date of publication.

para. 324

(1) If the limited company enjoying a majority participation (possessing the majority of shares) should fail to comply with its liabilities which para. 323 regulates, it may exercise its shareholders' rights within the controlled limited company only in compliance with the provisions for the case of acquiring a significant participation (significant part of shares).

(2) The acquiring of a majority participation (the purchase of the majority of shares) shall have to be published in the Official Gazette.

para. 325

In the case of majority participation (owning the majority of shares),
(a) the controlled limited company may acquire additional shares of the limited company possessing the majority of its shares (majority participation) and may acquire neither by purchasing nor by subscribing for shares, and may not exercise its right of voting due to it on account of its already existing shares;
(b) The same person may simultaneously not be a member of the Board of Directors and the Supervisory Board of the limited company enjoying the majority participation (possessing the majority of shares).

para. 326

(1) Within 90 days after acquiring the majority participation (the majority of shares), the limited company possessing the majority participation (the majority of shares) shall have to perform, upon the request of any shareholder of the controlled limited company, the following acts, corresponding to the selection of the said shareholder:
(a) He shall have to purchase the shares at least at the tender price or
(b) he shall have to pay in advance a dividend of the predefined extent.

(2) Omission of the term indent (1) has specified involves the loss of the right.

(3) Should the controlled limited company implement a business policy that is continually deleterious from the aspect of its own interest upon the influence of the limited company possessing the majority participation (majority of shares), upon request of creditors representing a least 20% of the debts of the controlled limited company, the Court may rule that the limited company possessing the majority participation (the majority of shares) shall undertake unlimited responsibility for the debts of the controlled limited company.

para. 327

A limited company owned exclusively or in majority by foreigners may not acquire any majority participation (the majority of shares) in another limited company. Upon violating this rule, the limited company may not exercise its shareholders' rights in the controlled limited company.

para. 328

(1) If the limited company possessing the majority participation (the majority of shares) has acquired more than three quarter parts of the shares of the registered capital of the controlled limited company, the Board of Directors of the controlled limited company may give instructions to the Board of Directors of the limited company under its direct control concerning the management of the limited company, and the controlled limited company shall be compelled to carry out any such instructions (a limited company under direct control).

(2) The controlling limited company shall have an unlimited responsibility for the debts of the limited company it directly controls.

(3) The direct control shall have to be entered into the Trade Register and published in the Official Gazette.

para. 329

(1) The shareholders of the limited company subjected to direct control may at any time require the controlling limited company to pay them a dividend of predetermined extent or to purchase their shares from them at the value existing upon making the decision, respectively that the controlling limited company shall exchange their shares against its own shares.

(2) The creditors whose not yet due claims from the limited company under direct control have occurred before the publication according to indent (3) of para. 323, may require, within 90 days after the publication, the controlling limited company to supply them with a security up to the value of their outstanding credits.

para. 330

(1) Mutual participation (interest) exists between two limited companies if each of them has acquired the shares amounting to more than one quarter part of the registered capital of the other one or if more than one quarter part of the votes are due to it in the general assembly of the other limited company.

(2) In the case of mutual participation (interest)

(a) the limited company earlier dispatching the notification according to indent (2) of para. 322 to the other limited company can retain the participation it has acquired from the registered capital while the other limited company shall have to decrease its participation to one quarter part of the registered capital;

(b) A limited company may exercise its due right of voting in the other limited company only up to one quarter part of votes which can be cast at the general assembly.

(3) If an influence also asserts itself by majority participation between limited companies of mutual participations, the rules of the majority participation shall apply to the relation between the two limited companies.

Closing provisions

Coming into force

para. 331

This Law came into force on January 1, 1989; The following laws, law-decrees and decrees were repealed:
(a) Law XXXVII of 1875 (Law on Commerce), i.e. the provisions still in effect of the said Law, except for paras. 291 through 298 on commercial drafts and paras. 434 through 452 on warehouse transactions,
(b) the provisions yet in force of Law V of 1930 on the limited liability company and the silent partnership,
(c) Law-decree 4 of 1978 on business societies, associations, companies and ventures and law-decree 34 of 1986 and law-decree 28 of 1987 modifying the first mentioned law-decree,
(d) law-decree 15 of 1981 on working teams,
(e) decree 9/1978 (II.1.) MT of the Council of Ministers on enforcing law-decree 4 of 1978,
(f) decree 30/1979 (IX.27.) MT of the Council of Ministers on the research-development production association and the research-development production society,
(g) decree 28/1981 (IX.9.) MT by the Council of Ministers on working terms and the relevant modifying decrees 5/1984 (I.17.) MT, 65/1985 (XII.30.) MT and 97/1987 (XII.31.) MT, all by the Council of Ministers,
(h) decree 43/1984 (XI.6.) PM by the Minister of Finance on enforcing decision 2011/1976 (IV.22.) MT by the Council of Ministers on agrarian industry associations as well as decree 43/1984 (XI.6.) PM by the Minister of Finance on enforcing the said decision,
(i) decision 2008/1978 (II.1.) MT.h on certain tasks relating to business associations,
(j) decree 28/1972 (X.3.) PM by the Minister of Finance on business societies, association, companies, ventures operating with foreign participation, as well as decree 7/1977 (V.6.) PM by the Minister of Finance modifying the former decree and decree 63/1982 (XI.16.) PM by the Minister of Finance,
(k) decree 22/1978 (IX.19.) PM by the Minister of Finance on the financial conditions of the foundation of business societies, associations, companies and ventures as well as the following decrees amending the former decree: 51/1980 (XII.12.) PM, 58/1983 (XII.29.) PM, 52/1985 (XII.28.) PM and 103/1987 (XII.31.) PM,
(l) decree 2/1980 (II.1.) PM-MüM issued jointly by the Minister of Finance and the Minister of Agriculture on the financial conditions on founding research-development – production associations and research-development-production societies and the following decrees amending the former one: 43/1983. (XI.12.) PM, 53/1985. (XII.28.) PM and 78/1987. (XII.27.) PM, all by the Minister of Finance,
(m) of Law V of 1930 on limited liability companies, ruling on the Forint values

defined by various provisions of the said law, respectively decree 10/1987 (IV.3.) PM by the Minister of Finance on the minimum extent of the registered capital of limited companies and of the nominal (face) values of shares.

Transitory provisions

para. 332

(1) The following societies, associations, companies, ventures, working teams operating on the date of enforcing the present Law:
(a) Business societies, associations, companies, ventures (Civil Code para. 568);
(b) (Business) working teams (28/1981. IX.9.) MT decree by the Council of Ministers;
(c) Associations;
(d) Joint ventures;
(e) Limited liability companies and limited companies
except for the exceptions which indent (3) provides, shall have to amend their respective deeds of associations (articles) corresponding to the requirements of the present Law up to December 31 of 1989 and shall have to notify the Court of Registration of the said amendment, respectively associations and joint ventures which have so far not been entered in the Trade Register shall have to demand their entry.

(2) The Court of Registration shall deem ex officio from the Trade Register any business society, association, company, venture which has failed to comply with the liability indent (1) requires, i.e. any such association and joint venture shall terminate (wind up) on January 1 of 1990.

(3) The provisions of indents (1) and (2) shall not apply to already operating limited liability companies and limited companies with fully or partly foreign interest which are based on international agreements or have been founded before January 1 of 1950.

para. 333

The entry into the Trade Register of working teams which have been established according to decree 28/1981 (IX.9.) MT by the Council of Ministers cease on January 1, 1990. The company working team may notify the Court of Registration, in the form of a written statement signed jointly with the company up to December 31 of 1989 whether it intends to convert itself into a business working team operating as an unlimited (mercantile) association/company, a business working team or a business working team operating under the responsibility of a legal entity.

para. 334

(1) Limited (deposit) partnerships established based on law-decree 4 of 1978, furthermore agrarian associations operating based on separate legislative rules

shall be terminated, respectively wound-up on December 31 of 1989 except for the case if they convert themselves into one of the business working teams or into another business society, association, company, venture which the present Law regulates.

(2) The registration in the Trade Register of Civil Law Societies shall terminate on January 1 of 1990. The Civil Law Societies which intend to conduct businesslike business activities after the enforcement of the present Law, shall have to notify the Court of Registration up to December 31 of 1989 their conversion into a business working team or some other business society, association, company or venture.

para. 335

Any conversion based on paras. 332 through 334 shall be free of any tax and dues.

para. 336

(1) Civil Code Societies established before October 1, 1988 for operating retail trade and catering establishments based on contract and lease may continue their operation until their contracts terminate, according to the provisions so far in force.

(2) Foreign trade companies operating on decree 32/1967 (IX.23.) MT by the Council of Ministers may continue their operation according to the rules which have been valid so far.

para. 337

The present Law does not affect any bearer shares acquired by foreigners before enforcement of the present Law in its quality as a bearer share.

Miscellaneous provisions

para. 338

The business society, association, company, venture the members of which (the founders of which in the case of a limited company) may include in their firm names
(a) the adjective 'state' if the members, respectively founders are exclusively state management organizations or other state bodies,
(b) the adjective 'cooperative' if the members are exclusively cooperatives or some other cooperative organs.

para. 339

The conversion of business societies, associations, companies and ventures into other forms of the said bodies as well as of the conversion of management/business organizations [Civil Code para. 685, point (c)] into a business society, association, company or venture will be regulated by a separate Law.

2. Act XXIV of 1988 on Foreign Investments in Hungary

In order to develop international economic cooperation, with special regard to the promotion of foreign functional capital in our economy and of the technical development in Hungarian economy hereby, granting foreign investors national treatment exempt from discrimination, the Hungarian Parliament has passed the following act:

Chapter I. General regulations

§1

(1) Investments of foreigners enjoy full protection and security.

(2) Foreign investors must be indemnified on actual value forthwith for losses resulting from contingent nationalization, expropriation or other provisions exercising similar legal influence.

(3) The state executes indemnification by way of the action of the administrative body that has made the provision. In the case of infringement of the law reconsideration of the administrative action of indemnification can be suited in court.

(4) The amount of indemnification must be disbursed for the person entitled to it in the currency of the investment.

§2

In the application of the present act;
(a) a foreigner is a juristic or natural person who is declared to be one by foreign exchange regulations;
(b) investments of foreigners in Hungary are economic corporations operating with foreign participation, economic corporations founded by foreigners, and acquisition of shares in an economic corporation by foreigners (hereinafter each called corporations operating with foreign participation).

§3

Corporations operating with foreign participation can be founded in the ways and forms regulated in the No. VI. Act of 1988 about economic corporations (hereinafter: Ec). The regulations of Ec. must be applied to these corporations – with the alterations and riders included in the present act.

§4

(1) Corporations operating with foreign participation are allowed to take part in the foundation of other economic corporations, to found other corporations themselves, and to acquire shares – with the restrictions included in paragraph (2) – in corporations already operating. The regulations of the present act – with the exceptions included in Chapter IV – are not applicable to these corporations.

(2) Stock corporations mostly or completely in foreign property are not allowed to take the majority of shares in other stock corporations.

§5

Legal supervision over a corporation operating with foreign participation is exercised by the court keeping the trade registry (hereinafter: registry court).

§6

If regulations are otherwise provided by international contract, the international contract must be administered.

Chapter II. Foundation of corporations operating with foreign participation, acquisition of share in operating corporations

§7

Foreigners are allowed to take part in the foundation of economic corporations, or in corporations as members if they are incorporated companies on the basis of their national right in Hungary or registered in the trade or firm register on the basis of their internal right. Any foreign natural and juristic person can be a shareholder.

(§7 taken out of force as of 1 April 1990)

§8

In corporations operating with foreign participation the state, corporate bodies, economic corporations devoid of legal entity, and natural persons are all allowed to take part as domestic founders or members, on the basic of Ec. regulations.

§9

(1) Corporations operating with foreign participation are allowed to be founded with the view of performing any sort of economic activity, excepting cases forbidden or limited by law.

(2) For the foundation of economic corporations mostly or exclusively in foreign property, for conversion into such corporations, for the acquisition of foreign majority shares in a corporation, a joint licence of the Minister of Finance and the Minister of Commerce is obligatory. This licence includes the licence of the foreign exchange authority. The licence must be regarded as given if the application has not been refused within ninety days of application.

(3) In the case of rates of foreign participation amounting to less than that indicated in paragraph (2) no licence of the foreign exchange authority or any other authorities is obligatory for the foundation of economic corporations or participation in corporations.

§10

(1) Application for licence [Section 9, paragraph (2)] must be presented to the Minister of Finance.

(2) The application must be presented

(a) in the case of foundation of new corporations by the Hungarian founder,

(b) in the case of exclusively foreign property by the foreign party,

(c) in the case of foreign share acquisition in an operating company by the corporation

in five copies in Hungarian. The application can be presented by somebody else by virtue of a commission; in the case of point (b) an inland deliverer must be appointed.

(3) The application must be inclusive of

(a) indication of the names (trade names), corporative form and residence of the Hungarian and foreign members (founders);

(b) indication of the form, place of registration and residence of the corporation and the description of their range of business;

(c) indication of the size of capital (assets, share capital) at the time of the presentation of the application in the case of operating corporations, or such data planned in the case of new corporations;

(d) the way of division of clear profit after taxation;

(e) exposition of the business policy of the corporation, with indication of data suitable for evaluation.

(4) The application must be supplied with the partnership contract (articles of association, draft of articles of association) in Hungarian, in the case of operating companies with amendments possibly necessary of the aforesaid documents.

§11

(1) In the matter of the application for licence the joint decision is pronounced by the Minister of Finance. Rejected decisions require reasons to be given.

(2) In case the application has been presented in a form or with contents other than stipulated, suppletory action is possible to be ruled in one instance within thirty days of presentation. Decisions must be passed in effect within sixty days of supplementation.

(3) One copy of the decisions mentioned in paragraphs (1) – (2) must be forwarded to the Registry Court.

§12

(1) Unless otherwise provided by international contracts, the foreign party is bound to pay its monetary contribution in convertible currency.

(2) Contributions other than monetary can be any negotiable goods with financial value, intellectual product and right with financial value.

§13

(1) If more shares have been subscribed than the number issued by the stock corporation and for this reason declinations take place, subscription of shares in corporations operating with foreign participation by publicly financed institutions or state banking institutions can be refused.

(2) Foreigners are only allowed to acquire registered shares. For the purpose of transferring bearer's shares to foreigners, shares must be transformed into registered shares. In the case of inheritance the bearer's shares of foreign heirs must be transformed into registered shares within one year of the distribution of the estate.

Chapter III. Conditions of operation of corporations

§14

(1) Corporations operating with foreign participation (hereinafter called corporations) are bound to disburse income tax for the enterprise. The assessable income is the profit realised by the corporation in the legal year in question. Corporations are not charged with any other form of obligatory payment for the benefit of the budget on the basis of their profits.

(2) The rate of income tax for the enterprise is forty per cent of the part of assessable income not more than three million forints; the part exceeding this sum falls under the rate of fifty per cent (calculated tax).

§15

(1) The corporations are entitled to all the tax allowances due to other national economic organizations.

(2) Further tax allowances in the sphere of income tax for the enterprise:

(a) if the proportion of foreign shares in the foundation capital amounts to twenty per cent or five million forints, the corporation is entitled to an allowance of twenty per cent from the calculated tax;

(b) if more than half of the corporation's returns from sales comes from the manufacturing of products or from the running of self-built hotels, moreover the foundation capital exceeds twenty-five million forints and the proportion of foreign shares in this is at least thirty per cent, the corporation is entitled to a tax allowance of sixty per cent within five years and forty per cent from the sixth year of the beginning of the sales of goods or services from the calculated tax;

(c) if the conditions mentioned in point (b) are in existence, and the corporation carries out activities listed in the supplement to the present act or regarded as of major importance from the point of view of the Hungarian economy, the corporation is entitled to a tax allowance of one hundred per cent within five years, and sixty per cent from the sixth year of the beginning of the sales of goods or services from the calculated tax.

(3) Tax allowances are available in the form of retention of taxes.

(4) The Council of Ministers can stipulate tax allowances of longer duration and of greater extent than those defined in paragraph (2) for corporations performing banking activities as well as those performing particularly substantial activities as those included in the supplement to the present act in the case of the existence of conditions as defined in paragraph (2).

§16

(1) In the case of the existence of conditions as defined in §15 paragraph (2) points (b) – (c), if the foreign member (shareholder) converts the whole or part of the dividends (shares) due to him to increase the foundation property, the corporation is accorded, available in the form of retention of taxes, tax allowances amounting to a sum equalling the tax due after the amount converted to increase.

(2) The proviso for the availability of the allowance defined in paragraph (1) is that the clear profit should be at least equal to the joint amount of the increase in the foundation property and the tax allowance due to it.

§17

In the case of investments accomplished by the corporation one hundred per cent of the value added tax due and previously calculated for that year is allowed to be retained.

§18

The capital goods made available for the corporation by the foreign member of the corporation in forms other than monetary contribution can be imported duty-free in Hungary.

§19

The corporation
(a) is allowed to acquire proprietory rights and other rights with respect to the real estate indispensable for the economic activities defined in the partnership contract (in the articles of association);
(b) administers its assets without restrictions within the limitations of the Hungarian law and the partnership contract (articles of association).

§20

(1) In the sphere of purchasing and marketing products, the corporation acts in compliance with the regulations concerning marketing of products and market supervision.

(2) Price calculations are determined by market conditions, within the limitations of the regulations about the prohibition of unfair economic activities and the imposition of unfair prices. If regulations establish official prices, those prices must be applied.

§21

Corporations are allowed to carry out activites of foreign, wholesale and retail trade in compliance with the regulations concerning national economic organizations.

§22

Rules concerning the defence of the quality of products and services are to be applied to corporations as well.

§23

Corporations are allowed to take up loans and handle their deals of money in compliance with regulations concerning other national economic organizations.

§24

The rules concerning other national economic organizations are to be applied to the accountancy, accounts of liabilities and assets and obligations concering the supplying of data of statistics as well as supervision by the state in the case of corporations.

§25

In the case of prolonged insolvency the rules concerning liquidation measures are to be applied.

§26

(1) The corporations are bound to disburse social insurance rates of the same measure as other national economic organizations on salaries and wages payed for their employees.

(2) Corporations are bound to disburse social insurance rates only after those foreign employees wishing to draw on the free national health service and social insurance services. This rule is to be applied to superannuation tax accordingly.

§27

Officials, managers, members of the supervisory committee and employees at the corporation can also be foreigners.

§28

(1) On the conditions of the employees' rights of labour, the Code of labour leg-

islation, as well as, within the conditions of that, the partnership contract (the articles of association) and the labour contract, whereas on their liabilities, the Ec and the Code of labour legislation is exemplary.

(2) The Code of labour legislation and other rules issued on the basis of that concern rights of trade union.

§29

Rules concerning wage regulation and the monetary interests of employees in managing position are to be applied to corporations if the proportion of foreign participation is less than twenty per cent or five million forints.

§30

With the exception of free territorial companies, the property of corporations must be denoted in forints and the registers of the corporations are to be kept in forints. The value of non-monetary contribution supplied by the foreign investors is to be kept in register on the basis of the currency of the foreigners' residence.

§31

(1) The corporations perform their transactions involving foreign exchange and foreign currencies conforming to the regulations concerning the national economic organizations.

(2) The exchange of forints to foreign currencies and of foreign currencies to forints with reference to the foundation, operation and liquidation of corporations, inclusive of the remittance of amounts made available for the corporations by foreigners on any grounds and also remittances by corporations for foreign members, is to be accomplished with the application of the official exchange rates currently determined by the Hungarian National Bank.

(3) Corporations are allowed to keep the monetary contributions supplied in convertible currencies by the foreign members of the corporations on their own accounts in the currency of the payment and are allowed to purchase capital equipments, spare parts and durable consumer equipments indispensable for their activities without restrictions. These sorts of capital equipments are allowed into Hungary to the debit of these accounts free of duty.

§32

(1) The shares due to foreigners from the profits of corporations as well as amounts due to the foreigners in the case of the liquidation of corporations or partial or complete sales of foreign property shares can be remitted abroad in the currency of the investment without restrictions on behalf of the foreigners, provided that the corporations are in possession of the reserves.

(2) In the case of the liquidation of the corporation, the liabilities resting with foreigners are to be performed before remittances.

169

§33

Leading foreign officials, members charged with business-management, members of boards of supervision and other foreign employees are allowed to remit abroad fifty per cent of their wages after tax received from the corporation, paid in the bank keeping the accounts of the corporation in the currency of their country of residence without restrictions.

§34

If rules of law prescribe licences to some activity for Hungarian economic organizations, the same licences are bound to be acquired by corporations, independent of licences prescribed in Section 9 paragraph (2).

§35

Unless other provision is made by this law, the regulations related to the economic activities of the corporations but having not a content of civil right cannot be applied, for they refer exclusively to state management organizations and cooperatives.

§36

Banks are allowed to vouch for the obligations of the corporations towards the foreign members resulting from their membership on the basis of the usual banking terms.

Chapter IV. Tax free territorial corporations

§37

(1) Corporations by foreigners or with foreign partnership can be founded on tax free territories as well, foreigners are allowed to take shares in such corporations. The foundation of syndicates is not allowed on tax free territories.

(2) The present act is exemplary for the foundation of tax free territorial corporations, for the acquisition of shares in such corporations and for the operation of these corporations, with the alterations and riders included in the present chapter.

(3) The conditions of the technical denotation of the tax free territories, the conditions of the establishment of projects and the conditions of performing activities on tax free territories, the regulations of passenger and goods traffic taking place with the tax free territories are included in the rules of law concerning customs regulations and formalities.

§38

From the point of view of the application of customs, foreign exchange and, with the alterations included in §39 foreign trade rules, tax free territories are qualified as foreign lands, foreign territorial corporations in the application of the aforesaid rules are qualified as foreign. In accordance with this, the rules regarding the regulation of prices as well as supervision by the state are not to be applied to tax free territorial corporations.

§39

(1) The regulations concerning foreign trade of international contracts compulsory to the Hungarian Republic as well as export and import regulations determined for particular relations or merchandise include tax free territorial corporations as well.

(2) Given licences of the Minister of Foreign Trade tax free territorial companies are allowed to perform foreign trade activities with merchandise and in relation of countries for which merchandise and in relation of which countries the Hungarian Republic have international contracts defining the sorts or amount of goods being exported or imported.

§40

To enter tax free territorial corporations into the trade register, decisions of the Ministry of Finance must also be enclosed stating that the real estates on which the activities of the corporations are planned have been declared tax free territories.

§41

(1) The books of corporations, with the exceptions regulated in point (2), are to be kept in the currency prescribed in the partnership contract (articles of association).

(2) The Minister of Finance has the right to order particular accounts to be kept in forints and the balance to be drawn up in forints.

(3) Corporations transact their businesses in convertible currency, excepting those regulated in §42 and occasionally permitted by the Minister of Finance.

(4) Tax free territorial corporations

(a) are allowed to keep their foreign exchange reserves up to the amounts of their foundation properties in national banks, their foreign exchange reserves over this in either national or foreign banks;

(b) are allowed to take up credit either from inland or from abroad without restrictions:

(c) are allowed to be free to dispose of their assets inland and abroad in convertible currencies.

§42

(1) Tax free territorial corporations purchase the amount of forints needed for the organization and operation in return for convertible currencies from Hungarian

banking institutions. They are bound to keep this amount of forints on accounts opened at Hungarian banking institutions.

(2) To the debit of the accounts described in point (1) are to be disbursed the following:

(a) rates and taxes,

(b) wages and other grants of employees and contributions imposed on these,

(c) duties imposed because of the use of territory and public workshop duties.

(d) the exchange value due for national natural persons and economic organizations without rights of foreign exchange, for retail trade acquisitions and building, mounting, repairing and similar jobs to be carried out on tax free territories, moreover for acquisitions and services not belonging to the range of activities of free trade corporations but necessary for the foundation and activities of the corporations.

§43

The Minister of Finance is allowed to give the concessions due to tax free territorial corporations partly or completely to non tax free territorial corporations operating with foreign participation, provided that the corporation does not carry out activities involving the forwarding of goods across the border. Such corporations can be classified as foreign.

Chapter V. Closing provisions

§44

In litigations concerning the partnership contract of corporations operating with foreign participation ordinary or arbitration courts in Hungary or abroad are to bring actions if the founders or the members of the corporation have made written reservations to this effect.

§45

This act comes into force on 1 January 1989; simultaneously point (c) of §11 of 1016/1985 /III.20/ decree of the Council of Ministers has been amended in compliance with §5 of the present act.

§46

(1) The regulations of this act

(a) are to be applied to corporations operating with foreign participation already operating at the time of the coming into force of this act, excepting the rules concerning licences (§10–11);

(b) are to be applied to cases already in progress with the modification that the ninety-day dead-line for the settlement of applications for licences (§9 par. (2)) is to be reckoned from January 1st 1989.

(2) Licencing charters issued before the coming into force of the present act remain in operation.

(3) Tax allowances authorized for corporations operating with foreign participation before the coming into force of the present act are allowed to be withheld from the taxes to the extent of the calculated taxes until the expiration of the allowances.

§47

The present act does not affect regulations concerning the foundation of banks and monetary institutions with foreign participation (§34 of Act II. 1979). The full value of the shares of such banks or monetary institutions, in contrast to paragraph (1) of Ec §264, are to be disbursed within three years of the registration of the corporation into the trade register.

Supplement to point (c) of par. (2) of §15 of the present act

Particularly important activities

(1) Electronics components;
(a) manufacturing active, passive and electromechanical components;
(b) manufacturing peripheries to computers;
(c) manufacturing electronically operated telecommunication main and sub-centres;
(d) manufacturing appliances of robot technics and services connected to their application;
(e) manufacturing computer aided planning and constructing systems;
(f) manufacturing electronic appliances and services connecting to them administered by the manufacturer, including the manufacturing of electronical consumer goods.
(2) Manufacturing components of vehicles.
(3) Manufacturing machine-tools.
(4) Manufacturing machines and equipment of agriculture, food-industry and forestry.
(5) Among machine-building elements:
(a) production of high precision cast, forged, pressforged prefabricated components;
(b) manufacturing components of general use and /quality appliances, valves, hydraulic and pneumatic units, up-to-date roller bearings and fittings, synthetic components suitable for increased and high strain/;
(c) manufacturing binding units;
(d) manufacturing tools and appliances;
(e) manufacturing technical ceramics.
(6) In packing technology:
(a) manufacturing wrapping material and appliances;
(b) manufacturing wrapping machines.
(7) In the field of medicine, plant protective and intermediary production:

(a) manufacturing new medicines;
(b) manufacturing plant protectives of new types;
(c) manufacturing medicine and plant protective key intermediaries;
(d) manufacturing preparations of veterinary therapeutics.

(8) Manufacturing products created on the basis of extensions increasing the convertible export of agriculture and food industry or decreasing their convertible import.

(9) The extension of national protein basis.

(10) Production of materials for propagation and breeding.

(11) In the field of developing the technology of the economy of materials and energy:

(a) manufacturing products produced on the basis of technologies producing materials enabling the formation of easier and more up-to-date structures /for example structural materials of great solidity, raw materials of great clarity, technologies of tempering materials/;
(b) producing elements applied in the field of process regulation, executing the continual measurement and supervision of the qualitative parameters of technological regulations;
(c) manufacturing appliances for technologies of waste cut saving materials;
(d) manufacturing equipments of processes utilizing by-products and wastage of large quantities /for example in forestry, plant cultivation, animal husbandry/.

(12) Long-distance communications services.

(13) In tourism:

(a) the foundation and management of institutions of thermal and medicinal tourism, if they are managed by the founder;
(b) restoration of historic castles;
(c) foundation and management of hotels of medium category /network/ if they are managed by the founder.

(14) Manufacturing products created on the basis of biotechnical and biotechnological processes.